PRAISE FOR

"Hamish proves that passion, love, and thinking outside the box have the power to change children's lives. He is a personal hero of mine. He's an educator I desperately needed in my younger life, and his interview was one of the most emotionally moving parts of *Humanity Stoked*."

—Michael Ien Cohen, director and producer, *Humanity Stoked*

"In 2019, U.S. schools need more solutions, not more problems, and *Relentless* delivers. A call to action, this book pushes *all* of us (students, teachers, administration and staff, families and communities) to 'go one more round' for our children. Award-winning educational leader Hamish Brewer reminds us that student success is built through love, persistence, empowerment, rigor, and most importantly, authentic relationships. Education stakeholders need to stop the blame game, face problems where they exist, and meet students where they are. Schools need to create opportunities, not more requirements. This book is no gimmick; it is a way of being. It is *real*. We must fight for all children. We must be all-in. So, roll up your sleeves. Show those tattoos. And be *Relentless*."

—John P. Broome, PhD, associate professor of education, University of Mary Washington

"In *Relentless*, Hamish Brewer shares a story of hope, love, and inspiration for making schools better. It is one part memoir, one part school-improvement guide, and a whole lot of motivation. The wealth of resources and strategies provided in *Relentless* can help any educator at the classroom or building level. Hamish challenges us to push boundaries and question the status quo in order to best serve our students, staff, and communities. You'll feel as though you are sitting next to him, sharing a cup of coffee as you are turning the pages. Hamish is doing the work and making great things happen because of his relentless pursuit to make the world a better place."

—Beth Houf, principal, Fulton Middle School; coauthor, *Lead Like a PIRATE*

"Hamish Brewer is exactly what's needed in education today. He is breaking the stereotype of leadership, getting results, and relentlessly fighting for all kids."

—**Paul Felder**, UFC fighter, sports analyst

"Ultimately, *Relentless* is not a book about tattoos and skateboards; it is a book about courage—courage to be yourself and courage to do whatever it takes to make a difference for your colleagues and for your students. Hamish Brewer has found his passion and his purpose, and he pursues it with reckless abandon. In this book, Brewer throws down the challenge for us to do the same. It is a challenge we all must answer."

—**Danny Steele**, educator, author, speaker

"*Relentless* by Hamish Brewer is the complete literary package. I've had the opportunity to visit Hamish at his school and see the *Relentless* mission in person. Reading about it gets me pumped up to be even more awesome for kids.

"Hamish lays the groundwork for educators to be themselves—to live the life and be the educator they want to be, not what they think society wants them to be. There's only one Hamish, but there is no reason for any of us not to take the *Relentless* strategies, ideas, energy—and Hamish's mojo and no-stop and no-quit attitude—to our schools. Buckle up. You're about to go on an amazing educational and life journey that you won't soon forget!"

—**Adam Welcome**, educator, author, speaker

"Hamish Brewer is a true maverick of education. He's the one who isn't afraid to do it differently, who ran into the fire, and who is relentlessly willing to challenge the status quo of an archaic system."

—**Jonathan Alsheimer**, teacher, speaker, author, *Next Level Teaching*

"The level of charisma and passion Hamish Brewer offers up when he speaks blows people away! With *Relentless*, he has translated the fire he releases on stage into print. I highly recommend this book for anyone looking to find purpose in their lives!"

—**Michael Bonner**, educator, author, speaker

"*Relentless* is a guidebook for anyone ready to truly disrupt the status quo. Hamish shares powerful stories from his personal and professional life that can elevate your own practices. It is an inspiring look at learning that will have you walking away ready to engage in this work at an entirely new level."

—**Jessica Cabeen**, Nationally Distinguished Principal, author, and speaker

"This book won't give you any programs. It's a story of hope and perseverance. It's a testament to what authenticity and love can do for school achievement and culture."

—**Eric Ewald**, principal, Van Allen Elementary

"Anyone who says 'it can't be done' clearly has not met Hamish. The title of this book could not be more appropriate. *Relentless* is the story of one guy's passionate approach to changing schools will both inspire you and push your thinking to new levels. Mount up! It's time to change things for our kids, schools, and communities."

—**Joe Sanfelippo, PhD,** superintendent, author, speaker

Changing Lives
by Disrupting
the Educational Norm

HAMISH BREWER

The Tattooed Skateboarding Principal

Relentless
© 2019 by Hamish Brewer

This book is available at special discounts when purchased in quantity for use as premiums, promotions, fundraisers, or for educational use. For inquiries and details, contact the publisher at books@daveburgessconsulting.com.

Published by Dave Burgess Consulting, Inc.
San Diego, CA
DaveBurgessConsulting.com

Cover Photo by Dustin Oakley
Cover Art by Daniel Kraft Alsheimer
Editing and Interior Design by My Writers' Connection

Library of Congress Control Number: 2019940215
Paperback ISBN: 978-1-949595-34-5
Hardcover ISBN: 978-1-949595-40-6
Ebook ISBN: 978-1-949595-35-2

First Printing: June 2019

DEDICATION

This book is dedicated to all the educators,
parents, and students with whom I have
been so fortunate and honored to work.

To every student who has struggled and
overcome, to those students still fighting—
know that you are just like me. Hope is real!
Your dreams *can* come true.

Dad and Mum, I love you.
We finally have peace!

To my family, you are my everything!

CONTENTS

Foreword xi

Life Doesn't Give You a Handout. xv

1: Skateboards, Backpacks, and Tattoos. 1

2: The Great Ones Go One More Round 27

3: Living for Love. 41

4: Lessons from the Fire Truck. 51

5: Think Opportunity, Not Obligation 67

6: Teaching 91

7: The Truth and Fallacies of School Improvement 115

8: A Nationally Distinguished Story 139

9: *Relentless* and the Fred Lynn Story 181

10: Live a Life of Passion and Purpose! 203

Acknowledgments. 213

More from Dave Burgess Consulting, Inc. 217

About the Author. 224

FOREWORD
by Andy Jacks, EdD
Virginia Principal of the Year
@_AndyJacks

Many people struggle with knowing their purpose. Those who have overcome this struggle and know exactly what their mission in life is are in the minority. One of those people is Hamish Brewer. I've never met anyone more focused on and deliberate about his vision for life and his school community than Hamish. He uses the word *relentless* over and over, as a personal and school mantra, and it's so fitting for his daily level of intensity and his sense of urgency. Hamish has made an amazing impact on my life, and I know that he has done the same for so many people around the world.

> *Success at anything will always come down to this: focus and effort. And we control both.*
>
> —Dwayne "The Rock" Johnson

Hamish and I have been friends for a long time, but our jump to better ourselves and our schools really began with a napkin in a bar in Nashville, Tennessee. While attending the National Association of Elementary School Principals (NAESP) annual conference, we met up each evening and rattled off new ideas and thoughts based on what we had learned from the day's sessions. Somewhere during our discussions, we bonded over our pent-up aggravation and our idealistic sense of *more* that we desired for our school communities. We sat around a table one evening and just lost it. We vented frustrations with the status quo. We challenged each other on what schools should look and feel like. More so, we dared each other to be something more, to own our destinies for our schools, and to stop blaming and start doing. If we wanted others to follow, then we needed to be better leaders and be true to ourselves—and stop worrying about what others thought we should be.

You can imagine the scene. We were sitting at a high-top table, having an intense conversation—our voices raised with passion and hand waving for emphasis. And like all amazing educator-spouses, my wife was right there in the middle of it, jumping in at times. Not satisfied with talk, she threw a napkin at us and encouraged us to write down our wish lists—and then to act on what we wrote. We still bring up that napkin all the time. To us, it represents a sense of vision and hope for who we want to be and what we want to accomplish. We started the conversation as colleagues and left as brothers who have had each other's backs from that day forward.

Intense love does not measure; it just gives.
–Mother Teresa

Hamish's passion for his school sweats out of him every day. It is evident in his daily routines and actions. Where many people spend their energy on the mundane systems for accountability, Hamish doubles down on building up relationships and positive momentum. And he isn't shy about using the word *love* with his staff and students. He tells them often that he loves them, something that makes many leaders uncomfortable.

Researcher and Boston College professor Andy Hargreaves says, "On school culture: It's hard to eat something that you've had a relationship with." As leaders and educators, we make the mistake all the time of "eating" our students and our teachers by creating obstacles, micromanaging, and instilling in them a general sense of negativity toward their work. The unintended, unintentional consequence is that instead of motivating people, we make them feel anxious, stressed, or inadequate. To avoid that, we must reflect on what we *do* on a regular basis and how our actions *affect* those around us. Do they help pull people together and motivate them, or do they make people feel worse about themselves and their efforts? In the same way, we worry too much about *what* they are doing instead of worrying about *how* they are doing. But it's one thing for kids to love their schools, and another thing altogether for them to love themselves. The latter comes from individual success and growth in their performance—from knowing that they are better and more successful now than when they started school.

Schools are notorious for adding measurement tools to gauge success, but so many times we focus more on the tool and less on the action. Talking with Hamish and seeing his routines reminds me to just go and do. Stop planning on what you will do someday and instead put that time to good use and go find someone, do real work, and just help them. When in doubt, give yourself to others directly, now. Not in plans or paperwork, but in your love and focus on their success.

Big results require big ambitions.
—Heraclitus

Many people have seen the flashy programs and amazing branding Hamish displays from his schools. What people don't always see is the constant focus that he and his teachers have on increasing achievement for their students. He will do anything to help a child be successful, and he has the results to prove it. Hamish has led major school transformations in culture *and* in student performance results. The best example of that was taking

Occoquan Elementary School in Woodbridge, Virginia, from the thirty-seventh to the ninety-fifth percentile for all schools across the state in just five years. The lesson here is that if anyone wants to change their classroom or school, don't think this only happens with fun cultural changes. Dig deeper and grind out better instruction and supports to ensure that students are showing these positive changes on assessments. That's where you really get buy-in—from students seeing these successes and then believing in their own futures.

I'm so excited to see Hamish's passions turn to print and to see this book continue his legacy of changing the game and disrupting the norm. Hamish's unique perspective, based on his life experiences, has made an enormous difference in my life. He reminds me every day to let go and be more of myself as a leader. People crave authenticity, and you can't be real if you aren't yourself, flaws and all. I challenge you as you read *Relentless* to reflect on your own story and your own dreams, to write those goals on your own napkin. Then, go make them happen.

LIFE DOESN'T GIVE YOU A HANDOUT

As a young child growing up in New Zealand, I thought my home life was pretty typical. We didn't have much, but I didn't need much either. It wasn't until I got older that I realized that some of the things that surrounded me, like the people who came in and out of my family's life and the drugs and amount of alcohol consumed around me and my two brothers, were not "normal." The older I got, the more things deteriorated. Then one day when we were teenagers, Mum moved out. I didn't know how to deal with the feelings of anger and abandonment that consumed me when my mother left. My plan was to bury the pain and never talk to her again—but that didn't make me feel any better.

Dad's income straddled the poverty line, and we struggled to make ends meet. We often went without in order to survive. Living on welfare and facing losing our house numerous times was stressful for all of us, but as the oldest son, I felt responsible—and helpless. I would seclude myself in my room and hide away in hopes that everything would be different when I came out. Our house wasn't big enough for all of us to have our own rooms, so to find some space when I got a little older, I built a bedroom in our garage. It flooded on rainy days and was susceptible to the weather in the winter months, but it was mine. Each morning after getting ready for school, I would stare at the pictures of swimming pools and exotic destinations I had taped around the mirror in my room and dream of a future far different from my reality. A map of the world hung on my bedroom wall, and as I learned about new places, I stuck a pin in the map. I tied strings from one pin to the next to create the path I would one day travel.

For me, school was not always the safe haven or place of inspiration it should have been. Sure, I enjoyed playing sports and hanging out with my friends in the school yard; in fact, I loved the camaraderie I felt in sports. But hiding behind the mask of confidence I wore with my friends on the field was a boy crying out for help. I struggled with the anxiety and heartache I felt at home (feelings I still deal with today). Academically, I found school to be difficult and oppressive, and I felt lost because I wasn't engaged in the academic process. I failed my high-school certificate exams and had to repeat a full school year. Floundering, I constantly worried about what would become of my life and future.

Not too long ago, I went back to New Zealand and visited with my old high-school principal, who remembered how hard my home and academic life had been. We talked about how my brothers and I had struggled in school and what we had gone through after my mother left us. I shared some of the creative (though not always legal) means my father found to pay the bills and feed the family—even if was five-dollar pizza night after night. My dad gave us everything he had. He taught us how to survive and how to love unconditionally. But he was also a man fighting—for his kids' benefit—to keep his head above water and make ends meet as he tried to overcome his circumstances and past mistakes. Things hit rock bottom for us all the night I fought with my dad as he was threatening to hurt himself. That moment, when we struggled on the floor in the hallway, summed up how shattered we all felt at that point. It was a moment I would never forget.

I knew then that something had to change.

CHOOSING A DIFFERENT LIFE

From an early age, I had felt a drive to do something great—to be something special. As a teen and young adult, I didn't know what that would be or how that drive would manifest itself, but I knew I wanted to leave my mark on the world. With all that had happened in our home, I knew I had a choice: I could wallow, hide, cry, and continue down the path my family had taken, or I could get up and do something. I chose—and still choose—to be *relentless* in my pursuit of making my mark. And this book tells my story.

I have lived, laughed, cried, and learned my way through life, all with a chip on my shoulder that has pushed me to beat the odds and prove myself to the world. I haven't always taken the easiest or most direct route, but everything I've learned and experienced along the way has shaped me into the person and educator I am today.

Throughout my career as an educator, I have been asked questions like these numerous times:

- "How do you do it?"
- "What's the program you use?"
- "How can I do what you have done?"
- "How do you get away with doing what you do?"

The straight-up truth is that my success in education (and life for that matter) is not rocket science; it's relationships. Everything begins and ends with relationships. In education, that truth applies to the relationships we have with all of our stakeholders: teachers, students, parents, and anyone else who has an opportunity to impact students. Being relentless in my relationships is all about being authentic and caring enough to say and acknowledge the things that are hard to hear. It's about being there for people and believing in them when they have a hard time believing in themselves. It isn't enough to lift one another up; we must hold one another accountable to remain focused on the goal at hand. When you acknowledge, respect, empower, motivate, inspire, and believe in people, you can move mountains. People want to be part of something special. Just like you and me, they want to leave a mark on the world. It's our responsibility, as educators and leaders, to help bring our students' and staff members' dreams to life. We can't do that without a relentless passion, belief, and strong, positive relationships.

Many people today, especially educators, live in fear of losing their jobs, expressing themselves, speaking up, taking chances, staying true to themselves, and being something they are not. They go through the motions behind closed doors—living to work rather than working to live. If that's you, it is time to come out from the shadows. Stand up and stand tall! Stop hiding your excellence, and instead, proudly celebrate it! Shout from the rooftops that you want to take on the world. Because here's the truth: You can be anything you want to be and do anything you want to do. Most importantly, you can be the difference for the kids in your life.

Relentless is a call for us all. It is an invitation to aspire to new heights. We all have it in us to be relentless. It's not something that I own or that you cannot be. My greatest desire is that you will choose to live your life with passion, integrity, and purpose every minute of every day.

Let this be your call. Choose today to be *relentless.*

1

SKATEBOARDS, BACKPACKS, AND TATTOOS

Back in the day, I spent a lot of time at CheapSkates, the skate shop in my hometown of New Lynn, Auckland, New Zealand. Shoppers came in and out of the store, but I would spend hours there daydreaming about being a skater—even though I was, at best, an average skater. After looking at boards, stickers, and clothes, I would head to the back of the shop where there was a couch and TV that was playing homemade skate movies. Sometimes other kids would be playing skateboarding video games, but I loved watching those videos. I aspired to be like the skaters I saw doing tricks on the screen.

Although I played a lot of standard sports, like softball and rugby, it was the "alternative" sports that called to me: skating, surfing, and rock climbing. I would spend hours reading and watching videos and magazines about surfing and skateboarding. I can still remember watching the very first X Games in 1995. I was hooked! I couldn't get enough of movies like *Endless Summer* and the inspiration I would draw from watching the crazy adventures that could be had from traveling the world. All I could think about was how that could be me traveling the world, surfing, and skating my way around, having fun, going on adventures! Through the years, skateboarding remained part of my life. I loved riding my board on the streets—even as an adult. (I can't tell you how many "No Skateboarding" signs I have ignored.)

In my fourth year of teaching, I organized a skateboarding show at the Laingholm Primary School in West Auckland, New Zealand, where I worked. West Auckland is a beautiful location on the West Coast, nestled just outside of the city, a sanctuary known for its beaches away from the hustle and bustle of the city. I had a connection with some of the local skaters and the skate shop, and I arranged for them to bring some equipment, so they could free skate and pop tricks while students watched. Some of the more experienced teachers thought the event would be a complete waste of time. They complained that it was unacceptable to have these "bad kids coming up to school and running roughshod over the playground area."

As it turned out, everyone had a blast.

The skaters thought that putting on a show, complete with loud music and half pipes, was the coolest thing ever. The teachers enjoyed the extra time in the fresh air. And the students *oooed* and *ahhed* as they watched the skate team do their thing. More than just being a great time, the event modeled for the students that they could be anything they wanted to be. This out-of-the-norm experience sparked connections and helped us build relationships with our students. It reminded us of the power that authentic and relevant learning experiences have for enhancing student engagement and ownership of learning. And by inviting the skaters to school, we advocated for *all* students. We sent a message that students don't hear enough: *You can pursue any and all activities your heart desires.*

That message is an essential one for students to hear. Unfortunately, the message they hear far more often comes from the "No Skateboarding Allowed" signs that hang on the fences and buildings at almost every school. I realize those signs are there for insurance and health and safety purposes, but what they tell students is that certain activities—and more to the point, people—are not acceptable at school.

That event early in my career set the stage for the kind of educator I would become. Eventually, I developed the reputation as the "relentless, tattooed, skateboarding principal." And it all started with my love affair with skateboarding and extreme sports.

BACKPACKING ADVENTURES

All the while, I had been sleeping on a mattress on the floor of the house that I grew up in. I was attempting to renovate the house so I could sell it, and I was consumed by dust, varnish, and paint fumes. I was struggling to maintain any form of balance when my best friend, Jason Ng, who was working with the school's board at the time, visited, and said, "Enough is enough! You are coming home with me." I credit Jason and his wife, Sue, with saving my life. They took me in and helped me get myself going in the right direction.

Teaching had been what I trained for and what I had done, but after five years, I needed a change. I quit my job as an elementary teacher. In keeping with my way of doing things a little differently (and having fun), I wrote my principal a resignation letter in the format of a retirement letter, explaining that I was retiring so that I could do the traveling I had dreamed about for so long. In reality, setting out on that adventure was my way of trying to figure myself out and deal with the issues and demons from my past.

I had spent a great deal of time working on my rock-climbing skills, training with Jason. I had grown accomplished at lead rope climbing, which is where you carry up your own rope and hook into anchors as you climb. I crashed at my brother Cameron's pad in Brisbane, Australia, for a few months after quitting my job and escaping from the mundane routines of life. One day while sitting in a café at the beach reading a climbing magazine, I came across an article about a climbing trip to Thailand. Immediately I thought *I'm going to go do this.* That very day, I bought a ticket to Thailand that would see me wheels up on a plane only a matter of days later. My plan was to go backpacking and rock climbing in Thailand just like the featured article in the magazine. (This was way before tourism really took off there . . . before the internet, and way before smartphones.) I arrived in Bangkok—alone—with a clear beginning destination in mind: Khao San Road, a well-known backpacking haven.

Unfortunately Khao San Road was not where I ended up. I found myself wandering the back streets of Bangkok, and I had never been so scared in my life. I thought I knew what being poor looked like. But it wasn't until I got lost in the ghetto in Bangkok that I really understood what it meant to live in poverty. I will never forget the smell of pollution or the sights of stray animals, prostitutes, trash piled everywhere, and people living in makeshift shelters no bigger than a cardboard box.

After twenty-four hours of no sleep, I finally found a safe location to rest. I tried to pull myself together, but my confidence was shot. I made my way to a shop that sold flights (no smartphones or internet, remember?) and booked the first flight home. There were no direct flights from Bangkok, so in my desperation to leave, I booked a trip with layovers in four different countries. It wasn't until after I purchased the ticket that it dawned on me that if I gave in to my fear and got on that flight, I would be running away—giving in. I realized that I would be allowing a bad experience to affect the way I wanted to live my life, which was with passion and purpose, not fear.

In life, we always have at least a couple of choices. I knew I could quit and go home, or I could pick myself up, dust myself off, and get on with the trip. I went with the latter and ended up skipping out on my tickets home. I still wanted to get out of Bangkok as soon as possible, so I booked a trip just outside the city to collect myself. That trip ended up going on for a number of weeks, and I had a blast. I put the location I had planned on climbing at on the back burner after I learned about an even better location, Railay Beach, from another backpacker I met on the trip. One hand-drawn map and an overnight bus later, and I had made it! The location was spectacular, and the climbing was even better. I knew I was a pretty good climber, but after watching the people around me, I realized I had entered a new league with some of the best climbers in the world in a place where the beauty made my head spin.

Living in an open-air hut with no running water never felt so good! I would go down each day with my bar of soap to bathe in the ocean water. We would climb in the morning and late-afternoon, as it was too hot during the middle of the day. And we spent the evenings partying under the glow of the moon and burning torches. Letting go, I experienced all that life had to offer, not needing to be anywhere—no schedules, no expectations, and no worrying about the clock. Living out of a backpack on the road gave me the solitude and freedom I had longed for—the solitude gave me a place to reflect and think where no one knew me or expected anything of me. It was liberating. For the first time in my life, I began to free myself of the demons that followed me everywhere.

Backpacking can be compared to the craft of teaching on so many levels: The creativity that goes into planning and preparing for an engaging, authentic travel experience is similar to that of preparing for instruction. The experiences we create inside our classrooms should draw on the same sense of wonder, excitement, and energy we feel when traveling. Along the way, we—and our learners—can explore, problem-solve, and think critically through the situations we encounter on the learning journey. And just as travel gives us opportunities to collaborate and communicate across cultures, communities, and borders, technology provides similar opportunities for the students in our classrooms.

Traveling the world, living out of a backpack for the better part of a year, and experiencing the freedom to make instant decisions based on my passions and interests was an amazing opportunity— one that I feel honored to have enjoyed. Some of our students may feel as if they are living their lives out of a backpack—but their reality doesn't hold the same kind of thrill. Those who come from different countries or cities may feel displaced rather than lucky to travel the world or country. Their families may have moved to survive (physically, financially, or both) rather than to follow passions or dreams. The stories I've heard from so many students through the years have taught me about true sacrifice, pain, trauma, and endurance, and they inspire me to be the difference for children each and every day! Just know when you look in the eyes of a student, don't assume you know; don't assume everything is okay and has been easy. So many of our students have lived such a full life that they make ours look pedestrian by comparison.

Why Not?

While backpacking in Thailand, I formed a friendship with a local Thai guy who went by the name of "Bing," and we spent a number of days climbing together. He showed me around the area, and we spent a great deal of time talking about life—which is what you do when you backpack around with total strangers. As we chatted, I shared my frustration of archaic practices in education and my desire to change the game, disrupt the norm, and ultimately make a bigger difference in the world and in education.

I firmly believe that people come in and out of our lives for reasons that we may or may not understand in the moment; there are seasons in life. That was the case with this friendship. It only lasted a few days, but the lessons Bing taught me have stayed with me and have influenced the way I teach and lead. One of those lessons was to ask a simple question: *Why not?*

Here's how asking *why not?* continues to influence my work today: When considering a decision, I encourage people to give the green light for teachers and students to take risks and try things because *Why not?!* Every time a teacher or group of teachers come to me with an idea, my answer is, "Okay, why not? Let's go!" In the work we do, unless an idea is negligent or unsafe, there's nothing we really can't or shouldn't try to ensure that our students receive an amazing, authentic, and relevant educational experience. As adults, we tend to play it safe or take the easier route, when maybe we should be throwing caution to the wind in the spirit of *why not?!*

THE POWER OF SHARING OUR PASSIONS

Even though I wanted to, you can't travel the world forever. While it would have been nice, my bank account couldn't support it! That being said, I was able to merge my two passions of teaching and traveling together by joining a culture exchange program for teachers through VIF (the Visiting International Faculty program). In 2003, I hung up my backpack in the state of Virginia and returned to the classroom. I felt a renewed sense of passion and purpose, and I wanted to share that feeling with students and other educators. I've been in education for over twenty years, teaching and serving as a principal, and most of that time, I've been known as the one who rides some version of a wheeled contraption around campus. (You should have seen the time I three-wheeled it down the two-story ramps in one of my elementary schools!) I never outgrew my love of skateboarding, and my passion for it has served me well in multiple ways.

At my current school, our facility is so spread out with long, imposing corridors. It seemed to take an eternity for me to walk from one end to the other. Instead of racking up the steps my first summer there, I decided to bring my longboard in and cruise down the corridors. Besides saving me time, it was fun! My staff noticed, and they loved that their principal was operating out of the box. They also thought our middle school students would be impressed. So, that summer, I tested their theory by skating to any meeting with a new student who would be joining us that fall.

> **Side note**: I believe that, regardless of the age of the students, the principal should welcome every new parent and student to the school. This first meeting sends such an important message to all the stakeholders. It lets parents know I care about their children. Taking time to meet with the students lets them know that I think they are important. And beyond that,

those one-on-one meetings give me the opportunity to tell the narrative for our school, including what my expectations are.

Every time I rode up on my board to greet the parents and students, they lit up when they saw me. Clearly, it was not what they expected. They immediately felt right at home and comfortable with me and, as a result, with the school. So with the initial control testing finished, once school started, I decided that I would continue to skate in the hallways with the students around—an incredibly bad move during the first days of school. I became the disruption, and my actions reminded me again that we must model and build the expectation for the students. Seeing the principal ride around in school on a skateboard was a shock—and maybe something I should have warned them to expect. It didn't take long for the students to get used to me riding around school, and now it is something that is a common occurrence.

Skateboarding is clearly one of my passions, one I love sharing with my students and staff. For years I have shared my love for traveling, backpacking, climbing, driving fast cars, and being a firefighter. I make sure to tell them both the good and bad that came with those experiences. I don't share those things simply because I like to talk about them. Talking about those experiences and the things I care about helps build relationships—and remember, relationships are where things begin and end in education.

Connecting with those around you by sharing your passions, interests, and stories helps them get to know you. (Students love and respect a principal or teacher that they know.) It's equally important that you get to know them. When you have to have tough conversations with students, knowing their stories and passions helps you understand where they are coming from and why they made the decision that they made.

The more I shared and modeled my love for skateboarding, the more students began to ask, "Can we bring our skateboards to school?" or "Can we ride our skateboards at school?" What I love most was that students who would often be overlooked because they were quiet, shy, or not disruptive came out of the woodwork to ask questions and talk about skateboarding. Our students' interest in skating fueled the skateboarding program at school. Before long, we saw how the skateboarding program was a way to advocate for *all* kids.

The reality is that kids who love skateboarding or alternative music don't always fit in to typical school programs. These kids are very quickly dismissed as disruptive or labeled as the "bad kids." That attitude has always ticked me off! I believe every person deserves to be able to express their individuality, interests, and beliefs uninhibited from society's stereotypes—especially at school. The archaic practices and policies that subdue creativity and discriminate against individuality create a toxic environment that we must all work to avoid or abolish in schools! It doesn't matter if a student is the "bad kid," the "rowdy kid," or the "quiet kid." You must find ways to relate to them. You have to humble yourself and get on their level. When you do that, you open yourself up to make a huge impact in their lives. You can't serve someone you believe you are better than or you don't respect as a human being.

Adding a skateboard giveaway program to our school was one way that we were able to reach kids who had previously lived on the fringes of anonymity or who tested the boundaries with their behavior. It created a new feeling of energy and excitement, and suddenly, students were lining up in hopes that their name was called to receive one of my boards. Corporations, like Vivint Solar, have donated boards to the program. Our students particularly love the boards with our school logo engraved on them.

When I launched the Mr. Brewer Skateboard Giveaway, the excitement went up another notch. Teachers nominated students who showed an interest in skateboarding or who may have needed a pick-me-up to receive a free board. Giving boards away is always a thrilling experience. I've seen tears of joy, utter shock, and pure excitement. I love it! Recently, a teacher from another state reached out to me to tell me about a student at her high school who was going through a really tough time. His skateboard had broken, and she had seen my skateboard giveaway program and wondered if I could help. The student was a huge skateboard fan and a stud skater. When I heard his story, I knew it was a no-brainer; this was my chance to impact students through skateboarding beyond my school or even my state. I sent an email to the teacher to let her know that I would send her student a skateboard. In return, she sent me photos of this student with his new board—a sight that could not have made me prouder. He was alive, and his fire was lit! The teacher even sent me video footage of him completely carving up his school and jumping vertically off some steps. We had made a difference in his life, and I hope he pays it forward one day.

Word got out about the skateboarding principal and our school's skateboard program and skateboard giveaway, which opened the door for interviews with news networks. As a result, I've heard from so many educators who have been inspired by my story to embrace and share their passion for skateboarding. One of those news show interviews even brought about an opportunity to fulfill one of my bucket list items.

After seeing a story about me, Michael Ien Cohen, a film director, reached out to me regarding a documentary he was making. I initially thought it was a joke (there are a lot of wannabe movie makers out there), but Michael was for real. He explained that he was producing a documentary titled *Humanity Stoked* about people who are making a difference in the world and sharing their thoughts and experiences through their love of skateboarding.

What sparked my interest was that the project was organic, gritty, and beautiful. Michael explained that everyone involved in the project was donating their time, skills, and energy, including some of the most well-known and influential skateboard lovers in the world. One of the people in the film was none other than one of my childhood heroes, Tony Hawk. When I heard that, my heart started pounding. "Michael, are you crazy?" I asked. "I am not famous like all these people. I'm not some kick-ass skateboarder or cool nonprofit owner. I'm just an educator doing my thing."

Michael insisted the documentary could not go ahead without me, that my contributions through skateboarding and the impact I was making on the lives of children and educators all around the world needed to be shared! So, of course, I said yes to the interview. I'm not sure if Tony Hawk is telling everyone that he is in a documentary with The Relentless Principal, but I can tell you this: I'm still geeking out over the fact that I will appear in a movie with one of my childhood heroes.

Humanity Stoked will be released in 2019, and it is just one more way that sharing my passion for skateboarding has helped me advocate for all students—and to prove that dreams *can* come true when you believe, persevere, and have a plan.

I'm not some kick-ass skateboarder or cool nonprofit owner. I'm just an educator doing my thing.

Serendipitous Serendipity and Silver Linings

Michael Ien Cohen
director/producer, *Humanity Stoked* and
founder of WhatStopsYou.org Foundation

If not for my misplacing a book while on a humanitarian film shoot in Cuba, Hamish and I would never have even met. It was a few weeks after the shoot, back in New York, when I took a break from editing to sit down to read. That's when I realized I had accidently left my book at the airport in Havana. I turned on the local news, never expecting all the events that would unfold if not for that careless mistake. That's how unexpectedly and how wonderfully serendipity works. Often when we least expect it, something amazing happens and a life-altering opportunity appears before us. That's why it's so important we keep our minds, eyes, and our hearts wide open. Of course, some people may have more opportunities and choices than others, but on one scale or another, we all have opportunities and choices in life. It is up to each of us to empower ourselves to take advantage of them. That's one of the critically important things Hamish helps kids to understand and to believe in themselves!

So there I was, sitting on the sofa, watching the kind of uninspired stories that are typical of local news broadcasts: water-main breaks, traffic jams, and weather reports. I normally prefer more substantive reporting, so I can't explain why I tuned in to the local news that night. Some would say it was the universe talking to me, whispering in my ear like a mysterious muse. Would you? I was about to change the channel when something caught my attention and made my eyes widen. It was a human-interest story about Hamish and the way he was making a difference in children's lives, not only by inspiring and empowering them but by inspiring the teachers to empower the children as well.

The more I watched, the closer I got to the edge of my seat, completely engrossed. Watching Hamish engage with the kids, I was reminded of my own lost and misguided youth. My heart was breaking open for these kids. Because of Hamish, they had what I so desperately needed from my teachers: inspiration, guidance, encouragement, self-confidence, to be challenged, and to be loved. Without that, the things we normally associate as the most important parts of education—the facts, formulas, rules, and old-fashioned structure—simply can't be processed with passion. "OMG *This guy is my fucking hero!*" I remember thinking to myself. Actually, I think I said it out loud!

At the time, I had just founded the WhatStopsYou.org Foundation, a 501(c)(3) public charity to help children much like those Hamish was helping. The foundation has a roster of amazing public speakers from the worlds of education, art, music, science, activism, business, and more, whom we could send to schools and youth groups in low socioeconomic areas, to give inspiring talks to the children who need it most. I knew Hamish was perfect for the roster, so I felt fortunate to have been in the right place and time to see his segment. I knew I had to meet Hamish. I knew I had to connect him to kids all over the country—all over the world—because I could see how he was empowering kids like I had never seen anyone do before. I quickly wrote myself a note for the following morning: "Google Hamish Brewer and ask him to join the foundation." I was stoked, but I had no idea how much better things were about to become!

I had just begun production on *Humanity Stoked*, a documentary with the singular mission of inspiring people to think more deeply about important issues that affect humanity. In the film, I was interviewing some of the world's top professional skateboarders, surfers, scientists, educators, musicians, artists, politicians, activists, humanitarians, and more. The surprising backbone of the film is that everyone in it, even the scientists and educators (really, everyone) shares a love of skateboarding; they are all skateboarders. It was a critical aspect because it made the film and its important humanitarian issues interesting and appealing to a diverse audience of kids and young adults. Some of the issues covered in the film were right from Hamish's wheelhouse, such as teaching kids how to overcome fear, the importance of being inspired, dealing with bullying in schools, and how we need to change the way we educate kids and the things we teach them. Instantly, I knew Hamish could have been perfect for the documentary, but alas, there was one massive roadblock. Everyone in the film is a skateboarder, and I remember asking myself, "How much better can this Hamish guy get? *What are the chances this guy is a skateboarder?*"

What happened next I call "serendipitous serendipity." Lo and behold, there goes Hamish; he's skateboarding down the hallway in the middle of a school, high-fiving kids, and getting them pumped! My jaw hit the floor as I said out loud, "No fucking way!"

The next morning, I managed to get Hamish on the phone, and we bonded instantly. There's something undeniable that's felt when two authentic people on the same path connect with one another. There's an authenticity and a sincerity that simply can't be faked, and when it's real, both people can sense it. Shortly after that introduction, we locked down a date to interview Hamish at his school in Virginia for the *Humanity Stoked* documentary.

The best was still to come, although Hamish and I didn't know it yet, and neither did Tony Hawk. As I began to prep for Hamish's interview by reading more about his life, I was stoked to learn about the strong and positive influence Tony Hawk had on him. I was blown away by Hamish and reminded once again about the power of being inspired. I knew I had to tell Tony about this guy. It had only been a month or so since I had interviewed Tony for the film, so I reached out and sent Tony a link to a great video about Hamish's story I found online by a company called FreeThink. I told Tony he had to see this guy, and that I wanted to do something special for him. I asked Tony to overnight me a signed skateboard, or at least a photo, made out to Hamish, so I could present it to Hamish during his interview the following week.

The following day, when Tony's overnight arrived, I opened the box and choked up pretty hard. It wasn't simply that Tony had decided to send one of his own skateboards for Hamish, or even the fact that he signed it for him. What got me was what Tony wrote: "To Hamish Brewer and all the lucky kids at the Fred Lynn Middle School—STAY RELENTLESS!! ~ Tony Hawk." It made me emotional because the moment I read it, it was clear that Tony had taken the time to actually watch the video and was as impressed by Hamish as I was. I couldn't wait to give it to Hamish.

Before the interview began, I left the wrapped skateboard with Nick Lang, one of my main directors of photography who's been tirelessly volunteering with me on the film from the beginning. About midway through the interview, the subject of Tony Hawk came up. Hamish was telling me how much Tony meant to him as kid and how Tony's example had inspired him to be a game changer in education, just as Tony had been a game changer in skateboarding. "Nick," I said, with cameras still rolling, "do me a favor and hand me that thing we brought down for Hamish, please." What followed next was so heartfelt, passionate, and meaningful. Fortunately for everyone, it's all on film and in the documentary. In fact, it's one of my favorite scenes.

Looking back, and thinking about Hamish and Tony, the sustained power of inspiring people and the wonderful ripple effect that can span generations becomes crystal clear. Tony had inspired Hamish all those years ago, and Hamish has been paying that forward by

inspiring thousands of children ever since. It was a tremendous honor for me to unite them both after all these years, and to acknowledge so much mutual love and respect.

BE WHO YOU ARE

I have been fighting against rules, regulations, and society norms since about the time I learned to walk. For me, the freedom to express one's opinions and individuality is part of what it means to live a purposeful, passionate, and intentional life. Unfortunately, sometimes expressing yourself as an individual—being you— comes with unfair consequences. As an adult, those consequences can include missed job opportunities and lost friendships, or simply the inability to experience life in a unique and pure way. For children, those consequences may manifest as teasing, bullying, seclusion, exclusion, and ridicule. All too often in life, we wait or look for permission to do and experience the things life has to offer. A great example of this is when people want to dance, but they almost freeze looking around waiting to see what others will do first. Instead of letting go and just dancing, they wait to see what the herd does—waiting on permission can lead you to missing out. You have permission. Let's go! One of the things I am proudest of is that my choice to live with passion (and to give the kids and adults around me the freedom to do the same) has empowered others to be true to themselves and live out their dreams.

But I wasn't always so confident. I can still remember asking for permission to show my tattoos as a young educator. In interviews, I would ask if the fact that I had tattoos would be a problem. The question I struggled with for myself was, *Should I be myself, or should I cover them up to conform to society's norms and not make waves?* Upon reflecting on that question and looking in the mirror, I challenged myself to stop asking for permission to be myself. I took on the attitude that, *If who and what I am is not good enough for you, then I am not who you are looking for.* For years, I felt completely comfortable in my tattooed skin—until I became a principal. With that new title, I fell back into the trap of trying to conform to what I thought others expected me to be as a role model and mentor to students and adults. I struggled for several months feeling as if I had to hide part of who I was. It felt uncomfortable, restrictive, and claustrophobic. Finally, I realized that by holding back, I wasn't being relentless. I found my freedom when I grasped the truth that I had earned the role I was in by being who I was; I couldn't turn my back on that. I had to be me and proud of who I was—tattoos and all.

Tattoos have long had a stigma attached to them. Some of that comes from tattoos being associated with gangs, violence, drugs, and rock and roll. I understand that some people use tattoos as a form of intimidation or exclusive membership to a club. But if that's all you think or see when you see tattoos, you're missing out. Tattoos are an art form. They tell stories and hold memories—a flower or angel to remind a person of a fallen loved one, or as my fellow firefighters often have, the number 342 to acknowledge the number of our fallen brothers from 9/11. In places like New Zealand, tattoos have deep meaning and connections beyond your wildest dreams. Tattoos, I believe, are like a silent conversation. So many more people than we'll ever realize have them hidden away by clothing and self-esteem.

Chutzpah for Kids and Teachers

Nicole Sweezy
teacher

I clearly remember the moment I realized Mr. Brewer would be like no other principal I had worked with before. He came into my room a week before school started like a ball of energy dressed in board shorts and tattoos and started offering his help with moving around tables and chairs. He even offered to help clean books. My mother and grandmother had come into school that day to help me set up my classroom, and seeing the confused looks on their faces, I introduced them to Mr. Brewer.

When he left, my grandmother turned to me and said, "The custodian seems very concerned about the progress of your classroom. Is he always this helpful?"

I laughed and told her, "That's not a custodian; that's our new principal."

Thinking this over, she smiled and said, "I like him. He has *chutzpah!*"

Chutzpah, as I had learned growing up, meant that you owned who you were without shame. After that moment, I began to realize that, based on the actions that Mr. Brewer took and the decisions he made, he does indeed have *chutzpah.*

Within Mr. Brewer's first couple of months at Occoquan, he gave us the "green light to teach on fire and not hold back." The message was clear. The instruction that went down in our classrooms and the interactions we had with our students and our colleagues all needed to be about the kids. I remember running to Mr. Brewer with new ideas for the classroom, wanting to get his approval before I got the ball rolling. Every time I approached him with a new idea, his response was the same: "What do you need to make this happen?" There was soon a new climate at our school, a climate among staff that there was no shame in being great because we were all focused on our being the best for kids.

And that's the climate others and I have grown accustomed to for the past seven years. Regardless of where we are, I know that when I walk into Mr. Brewer's office with an idea that's best for kids, he has my back.

Our students' tattoos may be invisible, but their experiences are etched into their lives just the same. Those indelible, internal marks represent their culture, their loves, their hates, their struggles, and their triumphs. Much like how education and instruction don't fit into square boxes, neither do our students. Life is messy and so are our students. Their "tattoos" prove this to us, but we love them regardless and without judgment. As educators, we don't choose or select our students; we take them all—tattoos and all. Just like we hope that society will see our tattoos and spare us the judgment, we must do the same for our students. We must allow them to express their individuality, discover who they are, and to not rush into adulthood. Let's give them the opportunity to experience the joy of living in the moment and the freedom to be who they are. *One of our most important responsibilities in school is to protect and advocate for our students' individuality and identity; it's their greatest gift!*

In New Zealand, we call traditional tattoos *ta moko*. It's a form of tattooing passed down through the generations, and the markings represent the Maori people, culture, and heritage. There has

One of our most important responsibilities in school is to protect and advocate for our students' individuality and identity; it's their greatest gift!

been a significant resurgence in the traditional practices of tattooing in New Zealand, with many people applying both Maori and Polynesian markings as a way to connect with their culture, family, and country. *Ta moko* has significant connections to the past, present, and future. It is a symbol of integrity. Upon experiencing the journey that one goes on with having *ta moko* placed upon them, there is an expectation that one represents oneself, family, and country in an honorable way. One carries not only one's own legacy but also the legacy of Aotearoa, New Zealand, and becomes *Tanagta Wheneu*—people of the land.

My *moko* have significant meaning; they are symbolic of my family and the area where I grew up. They are very meaningful for me, telling deep stories of my past that have set me free into the light and given me the ability to express myself and pull through some of the hardships I have experienced. They are a constant reminder to live in the light, to dream, to travel the world, and to live my life with purpose, meaning, and love. As an extremely proud Kiwi, my *moko* serve as a constant reminder to advocate for those who cannot do so for themselves, to be the difference, and leave a mark on the world for good. *Ta moko* is never done. The story is never ending. My work connects the past, the present, and the future—even today, the work isn't done; the story is not finished. My life experiences will continue to dictate the opportunities, dreams, and realities that come next.

When I feel particularly connected to an audience while I'm on stage—when I feel their energy and respect—I will often perform a *haka* at the end. A *haka* is a traditional war dance that is performed today to represent the ultimate gift and sign of respect to the people around you. It is often done before sporting events, weddings, and funerals as the ultimate sign of respect. As a child growing up in New Zealand, you practice this and imitate the performances of the *haka* from your heroes such as the rugby players

"I never had a principal who looked like you."

Lindsy Stumpenhorst

principal

I had a few discreet tattoos, but when I considered the possible placement of a new piece of art that would be more visible, I was concerned about what my school families might think. So I reached out to the most successful and tattooed principal I knew: Hamish Brewer.

After I asked several questions about having visible tattoos as a principal, Hamish said to me, "Lindsy, let's hope at the end of the day, you're going to be judged by your work and the person you are. If your families love you now, they'll love you tomorrow. Be proud of you and your beliefs."

When I pushed Hamish a little further about his experiences, he continued, "Don't worry so much. You've probably already upset the ones who are going to be upset by it, anyways. We give so much of ourselves; it's important to do something for you."

It's common for humans to pass judgment on people, especially those in a position of leadership. Being a young, female principal from a rural upbringing has its own set of unfair expectations.

When a new family comes to our school, I always give the tour. I'm incredibly proud of our accomplishments and love sharing! Not long ago, after I finished one of these tours, the dad asked when they could meet the principal. Upon noticing my grin and extended pause, he said, "Wait. You're the principal? I never had a principal who looked like you."

I do rather enjoy being underestimated.

from the All Blacks (a few of my favorites were Wayne "Buck" Shelford, Sir Michael Jones, Josh Kronfeld, and Richie McCaw). When performing, you leave it all on stage: you muster up your energy and attitude by calling upon your ancestors, family, and pride in your country to stand with you and come out through your body in an explosion of pride and energy! *Kia kaha* (never give up, never give in)! As a young teacher in New Zealand, one of my favorite things to teach was *kapa haka*—the *waiata* (songs), *haka* (dance), and traditions of Maori culture, including artwork and weaving to our children. Over the years, I have been fortunate enough to start or help start *kapa haka* groups and school connections to local *iwi* (people) through representation on school boards and to have also had the experience of working a few times in a full-immersion setting for Maori culture back at my old school in Owairaka.

I share all that to say this: We must be true to ourselves. My tattoos, my *moko*, my heritage, my hurts, and my passions all combine to represent who I am. Our experiences and how we choose to face them all shape who we are. We are all individuals, and by expressing our uniqueness and sharing it with others, we empower others to do the same. So many educators have thanked me and have told me my choice to be who I am has inspired them not to hide their tattoos, or love for skateboarding, or *whatever* is important and meaningful to them. I love that! As educators all around the world find the courage to express their individuality, they become the best versions of themselves—and the children they teach benefit.

It's Okay to Be Different

principal

Hamish has given us all a license to disrupt the expectations in education. He has shown the world that school can and *should* be a fun place for all people. He has paved the way for *different*, and that is exactly what our kiddos, teachers, and families need. They don't need a boring guy in a suit sitting in his office who does not connect with anyone. They need people like Hamish: people who are willing to challenge the way we have done things for decades, to break that mold, and start doing things that work for all people!

While I could never do what Hamish does, he has forced me out of my comfort zone and has helped me to realize many areas where I need to change and improve. I will always be a work in progress (we all are), but I got my jumpstart from Hamish, and for that, I am so deeply grateful. If not for Hamish, I would never have decided on a tattoo honoring my family and Jesus on my wrist. Again, he has paved the way for us all to be different, to be who we are meant to be, and to be the best for our kids and own families. He gave us all permission to be ourselves. Don't stop pushing, Hamish. Keep changing the world! Your impact is far bigger than just the schools you serve!

2

THE GREAT ONES GO ONE MORE ROUND

B eing a great educator is hard work. By comparison, the solitude of living on the road, in a place where no one knew me or expected anything of me was so liberating. For the first time in my life I began to feel free of the demons I had been running from. But educators don't often feel that sense of liberation. Even on the best day, the pay is not good, data drives the wrong decisions, and testing, paperwork, and archaic practices and policies are enough to make anyone feel like giving up. Throw in the days when it's cold and dark outside when you leave for work and cold and dark when you return home, and the days when you feel like you can't catch your breath because you have been hurdling upset parents and politics all day, and you can see why people are tempted to settle for average—or just quit.

The truth of the matter is the inspiring work that we do is hard work. It takes dedication to master your craft. Ensuring that every day is an opportunity for great instruction requires intention. It's not easy, and it doesn't come without sacrifice. The sooner we acknowledge and embrace this truth, the sooner we can liberate ourselves from the toxic internal and external factors we struggle against as we fight to make a difference each and every day.

In our roles as leaders and as educators, there will be plenty of circumstances that are going to knock us down. When we hit those hard days, those hard weeks—or years—we have a choice. We can throw in the towel, or we can get up and choose to go *one more round*.

Going one more round is about living with integrity and character. It's about living into your *mana* (power) and acknowledging the amazing opportunities that come with being a relentless educator. That's why I choose to get back up. I've learned that for as many of those experiences that throw you off your feet or knock the wind out of you, there are just as many amazing experiences that can inspire and fuel you. If you get back up, you can use those experiences—the good and the bad—to push yourself to be and to give your best to the children in your life. It's worth it, because we have the greatest job on the planet!

You won't keep getting back up if you don't have a plan. Your effort has to match the dream, and dreams do not come true without a plan. Eventually, you'll just get tired and give up. So I want you to really think about how you are going to attack every day and maximize the opportunities you have to make a difference *every day* as a leader, educator, and professional.

Your effort
has to match
the dream,
and dreams do
not come true
without a plan.

I want you to answer these questions for yourself:

What does "one more round" mean to you?

How far are you willing to go for those around you, those you lead, and most importantly, for children?

How far are you willing to go as a colleague, friend, or spouse?

Do you put those around you first, or do you cast a shadow that detracts from the team and children?

What do you do to put the team and those around you first?

How do you show kindness?

_____

_____

How do you uplift those around you?

_____

_____

_____

What do you do to leave your school and those around you better than you found it/them?

_____

_____

_____

All of us will have different answers to those questions based our experiences, values, and perceptions. We don't have to be the same as anyone else; we simply have to commit to being the difference-maker in others' lives—however that looks. It's that commitment that separates the average and good educators from the great ones.

9 HABITS OF GREAT EDUCATORS

Great educators are the ones who leave a legacy. They are always chasing something higher and bigger than themselves. They push themselves and the people around them to live with passion. These are the kind of people I surround myself with in my school—and in my life. The greats are different; they are game changers, and they are who our schools need each and every day. So what does it take to be great?

Humility

As a high-school athlete, I experienced success, and I remember a teacher (whom I did not like), giving me one of my life's greatest lessons. He said, "You will never be great while you do all the talking about yourself. Let others beat the drum for you; let others blow the trumpet for you." His message resonated with me then and has stuck with me ever since.

The great leaders, the great organizations, and the great schools put the team first. They leave their egos at the door and value the success of the team over any one individual's success. When that happens, they move mountains for one another.

Attitude

You get to choose your attitude. You own it. Your attitude is your responsibility—no one else's. Before you go through the doors of your school each morning, think about the opportunity that you have each and every day—the reasons you wanted to be a leader and educator. If you are not thinking about the opportunity, then you are focused on the obligation of a j-o-b, and that is where average lives. If you are leading and teaching for opportunity, you are on fire!

Your attitude is one of the few things that is within your absolute control. As educators, we spend way too much time trying to control the things we have no control over. Release yourself from the shackles of toxic behaviors and conversations that weigh down your attitude. You know the kind of conversations I'm talking about. Most people do an amazing job of talking about other people or issues. They are great at bringing problems to the table. But there are relatively few people who talk about solutions or talk about being the answer to an issue.

If you are leading and teaching for opportunity, you are on fire!

I challenge you to hold yourself to a higher standard. You will feel liberated and stress free when you stop surrounding yourself with negative people and behaviors, when you stop trying to control the things you can't. As I tell students, do not let anyone steal your future. If the people around you do not make you better, then cut them loose!

Living in fear of what others may think is another thing that can affect your attitude—especially when others look at you like you're crazy for coming into the building so happy or sharing how much you love your job. Just because other people hate their job (or life) doesn't mean you can't love yours! That's on them. Don't let their negativity slow you down, and don't worry about upsetting those around you by striving to improve yourself and your work. Cut negativity loose!

Persistence

It's easy to be great in September. That's just the first round. But your legacy is not built on what you do in a week at the beginning of the year. It's what you do when the work gets hard that counts. Commit to never giving up. Don't look at failure as a step back; instead let it be an opportunity to learn and grow on the way to success.

Accountability

Teams and individuals that reach greatness only do so when their actions—not just their words—move them toward success.

Let's hold each other accountable for our actions and words. Let's hold each other individually and collectively accountable for our team and school success! Let our actions, not our words, be what define us. Let's hold each other accountable, most importantly, for children!

Sacrifice—Together

Every team is stronger when its members sacrifice for one another and chase greatness together. We need to stand fearlessly side by side and stare down the challenges together. If we truly want to accomplish something great, we must commit to going one more round for the teachers and leaders around us. *Together* we can move entire communities and schools. *Together* we can go further, faster, and bigger than others can even imagine.

When I think of sacrificing for my team, I ask myself what am I willing to give up and what I'm willing to die for to be the difference in the lives of the people in my school community.

Focus

We all have personal hurdles and commitments. That's life. But when we are on our school campuses and working in the trenches alongside our fellow teachers, leaders, and students, let's make that time count. Let's choose to tune out the noise and outside distractions and do everything in our power to help children be the best that they can be.

No Fear of Failure

Failure is only an idea; it's how you think or feel about something when it doesn't work out or wasn't successful *this time*. But failing once doesn't mean you can't continue to work on a way to succeed and get it right. The greats refuse to give in to the fear of failure. Instead, they use failure to push them to find a solution. Choose to learn from the lessons failure offers and strive to do better next time around. Remember, there are no shortcuts to success. Winning and achieving greatness always require hard work.

So many people fail and give up because they are not all-in; they don't go after it with all their being because they truly don't believe it can be done. The greats believe and are willing to give it all they've got. Believe in your school and students like that, and you will do whatever it takes to define the outcome.

While you are working the solution—chasing it down with passion and vigor—stay true to yourself, your mission, and the vision for what you want to accomplish. I'd rather fail being who I am than fail being someone people wanted me to be. But really, I never think I am going to fail, because I always have one more round. I simply refuse to give up.

No Excuses!

No excuses. We don't blame children! Blame is not a solution for improvement. Great educators and leaders don't make excuses. They don't look around and point the finger. When you are looking for the person responsible for your situation, look at yourself in the mirror. You own your actions and your responses—no one else does but you.

If you're waiting on someone to come with help, help ain't coming—*you* are the cavalry. Let's go; the time is right now! It's easy to think, *If only I had more time*, or *What if they came to school more ready and prepared*? Those are all excuses!

Character

The willingness to go one more round is all about character. We are defined by who we are and what we do when we think no one is watching. If we truly want to move our communities and schools to greatness, we have to model and teach the students the character traits they need. You can do that by standing up for what you believe in and showing conviction for what you do. People will always rally behind someone who shows that kind of character. Character is standing with integrity—with *mana*—advocating for all.

If you're waiting on someone to come with help, help ain't coming—*you* are the cavalry.

TEACHING KIDS TO GO ONE MORE ROUND

Students today are used to getting everything instantly. For good, bad, or worse, this reality has removed so many of the lessons that come from taking risks, facing adversity, failing, and losing. When everyone gets a trophy all the time, we deprive our kids of the struggle it takes to learn perseverance and grit. So many of life's greatest lessons come from failing and losing. As the saying goes, you've got to lose one to win one sometimes. Facing adversity teaches us to not quit, to get back up when the odds are stacked against us, to fight, and to not give up when walking away would be the easier option. Adversity teaches us to go one more round.

When I was a teacher, I would hang a sign in the front of the classroom that read, "Pride in Performance." This saying superseded all excuses. If students couldn't say they were giving their very best each and every time, then they weren't taking pride in themselves, their performance, or one another. One of the core values in our class was to take pride in fighting for each other's success. That fight began with their personal space and then extended to the people closest to them, and finally to the entire class. We would talk about how far we were willing to go for one another, about what we wanted others to think of us as individuals and as a group. In these discussions, I would ask the students if they were willing to fight for one another to ensure we were all successful. Would we go one more round for one another? The answer was always *yes!*

Every school in which I have been a principal, I have a mural of a boxing ring painted with "One More Round" on it. It's a way that we challenge our students to fight with their minds, hearts, and souls. In my school, I want students to learn the importance of character. I want them to develop the grit that gives them the strength to face adversity and challenge head on—because there *will* be times when life humbles them. I want to prepare my kids mentally so that they don't quit. I want to teach them that when (not if) they fail, the way to win is to get up and keep trying until they find success. As educators, we are all in the business of teaching kids to not quit, to not give up, to not expect a trophy. Life doesn't give you a handout, and it doesn't just give you a trophy. We need to teach kids how to persevere in the face of adversity. It's okay to put some adversity back in school in order to teach students how to overcome and how to go one more round.

The words students see and hear in our schools shape how they think. That's why my teachers and I ask our students, "How many more rounds do you have? Are you willing to try again, to try until you can't try again?" We teach our students that no matter what, we will not run; we will not go silently into the night. We will come out fighting for what is ours. We will not let anyone steal our future from us! I love the fact that I can walk into a classroom and ask the students, "Are we average?" and they respond, "No, we are relentless." "How many rounds can you go, or how many do you have left?" and they respond, "I got one more, Mr. Brewer!"

Many of the students I work with have spent most of their lives experiencing and seeing failure all around them. They are from broken families; many of their parents are high-school dropouts, and their families struggle to keep a roof over their heads and food on the table. School is hard for many of them. An attitude of compliance and survival surrounds them. But I have never met a parent who doesn't want what is best for their child. When I look into the eyes of my students' parents, I can see that their hope and expectation is that I will do everything humanly possible to ensure their child is chasing their very best. They *want* their child to learn to go one more round.

One more round is not a slogan or New Year's resolution; it is an everyday thing. It's a *you* thing. Life is not always fair, and it's not going to give you a handout. When people are looking around for help, when they are down on their knees wondering whether they can go on, or they are in the classroom and they have been fighting every day—giving it their all—they are looking for someone to step up and be the answer. They are looking for a leader who will show them how to go one more round. The leader doesn't have to always be the principal. Regardless of your role, you can empower others when you lead by example. As you step into the fight for your school and each other, bear down, grit your teeth, and clench your fists. It's go time!

Let's go one more round for each other!

Let's go one more round for greatness!

Let's go one more round for children!

3

LIVING FOR LOVE

Growing up, I didn't hear the words *I love you* enough. Maybe that's because life was crazy busy. Living in survival mode, we didn't take the time to stop and catch our breath, much less say *I love you*. After a while, those words seemed uncomfortable or unnatural in my family.

We all regret that now. These days, we are working to make up for lost time. My father and I finish almost every phone call or visit with the words *I love you*.

I believe that, in our schools, we face the same problem as my family did with those words. We rarely, if ever, talk about love overtly and openly. Something as simple as giving a struggling or upset student a hug can seem complicated. I'm amazed at how many educators have told me how scared or uncomfortable they feel using the word *love* with their students or staff. As a child, I needed to feel loved. So I decided years ago that if the day ever came that I couldn't hug a child or tell my students I loved them, then that would be the day I should quit.

By talking about love often and encouraging my staff to do the same, we are helping to make the word *love* feel more acceptable and normal in schools than it's ever been before. I start each school day by reminding our students on the morning announcements that "If somebody didn't tell you today that they love you, Mr. Brewer is telling you that he loves you. I love you!" When I first came to this middle school—which was considered one of the toughest in Virginia at the time—people thought I was crazy for beginning the day by declaring my love over the PA system. Naysayers snickered or simply stared at me in disbelief. Some people said things like, "These kids don't care about that," or, "They don't want to hear it," or, "It won't work."

Well, I'm here to tell you that saying the words *I love you* every day has made an impact in our school in countless ways. So many of my students do not have anyone else telling them they are loved. As a male principal, I know that I am a role model for so many of my students, who may not have a positive male example at home or in their neighborhood. I make sure they know I'm there for them and that I love them. It's a responsibility that I take incredibly seriously because I know what it's like to not have someone in your corner telling you they love you. So I make sure they hear it from me all the time. The funny thing about it is if the kids don't hear me on the morning announcements, they wonder where I am. The fact that they miss hearing me tell them I love them proves my point: It matters! The kids *do* pay attention, and they love feeling loved. I can walk down the hallways at school now, and the kids will openly tell me that they love me; there's no shame or discomfort with those words that come from the heart.

I challenge you to introduce the word *love* into the everyday vocabulary in your school. I've heard from so many educators who have done this and seen powerful transformations in their schools. When kids know that you love them and are there for them, it makes a difference in the way they think about school—and about themselves.

Our children need to feel loved, and far too many of them don't feel that love at home. When they come back after the weekend or a holiday, you do not know what they have been through while they were away from school. Often, time at home can be lonely for students. Many of them (believe it or not), look forward to being at school. When you greet them in the morning, your smile or hug might be the first one of their day. Our goal as educators must be to make schools a safe place where children feel protected, nurtured, and loved—and that starts by openly expressing our care for everyone in our schools.

I want you to stop what you are doing *right now* and tell someone that you love them. Maybe it's someone special whom you haven't said *I love you* to for a while. Tell them now! If you are reading this at school, stop and tell a student (or your next class) that you love them, and just watch what happens! My bet is that you'll see a smile. Some people may giggle or may not know what to think. Some may say, "I love you, too!" or "Okay . . ." It doesn't matter what their response is because you will have just given them the gift of love. They'll feel a sense of happiness, pride, or energy, because love lifts people up!

If we make love the center of our school, we will win every time because love turns us into a family. When you create an environment built on love and family, you create an opportunity for trust, respect, and risk. Nothing warms my heart more than to see

If we make love the center of our school, we will win every time because love turns us into a family.

the transformation that takes place when students and staff show respect and love for one another. You can see love in the small things, from random acts of kindness that make someone's day to helping students pick up materials they dropped in the hallway, to offering a smile when someone needs a pick-me-up. And when people in our families make mistakes, we love them anyway. I'll even tell my kids when they've made bad choices, "I don't like what you did, but I still love you." Families take care of one another; families lift one another up and hold each other accountable. That is the kind of experience I want for all students.

That love must show up in every interaction, including those we have with our students' parents. When parents know that you love and care for their children, they will be more willing to accept and listen to constructive feedback. I found when I stopped preparing myself for a fight with parents when they came in and, instead, saw them as they saw themselves—as advocates for their children—I was able to better understand their point of view. I could see that their concern comes from the heart. When dealing with parents, ask, *How can I help?* Letting them know that you want to partner with them on behalf of their child will completely change the trajectory of your encounters with parents.

You can build up goodwill with parents and show your love for their children by making sure they hear from you when things are good—not just when there's a problem. An easy way to do that is through good-news calls. I have been making positive phone calls home for years, and every one is rewarding. A few years ago, this concept caught on with its very own hashtag #goodnewscalloftheday. It's amazing how transformative a positive phone call home can be for the student and their parents. We call home together and let the parent know something good that's going on for the student. I always wrap up the call by having a student say, "I love you," to their parent. When the parent responds with, "I love you," I always chime in and say, "I love you too!"

LEGACY

Like a lot of kids growing up in New Zealand, I wanted to be All Black. This rugby team inspired us to run around on cool winter mornings, where the fields were covered by fresh dew, and my toes ended up feeling like icicles because we would play in bare feet. The All Blacks were like giants, superheroes that we all wanted to emulate. We would do our best to learn their moves and employ them on a Saturday morning.

There wasn't one of us who couldn't perform the mighty Maori war dance—the *haka*—which was done at the beginning of the rugby match. The dance is a sign of respect for the opposing team's players—and it lets them know that they are about to go head to head with you and that you are going to play with every last drop of your being. In essence, you're saying, "I am coming for you. Be prepared to go to hell and back during the next eighty minutes because I will not let up until the final whistle."

What made the All Blacks so powerful was their ethos. That was their legacy. It didn't matter if a player was the most senior on the team or the rookie. No one was more important than anyone else on the team. Each person gave everything of themselves to ensure the team was successful—and they never gave up. One famous All Black once said, "I'd piss blood before coming off [the pitch]." That's the level of commitment and relentlessness that we should demand in our schools. (One of the books I give any new staff member is *Legacy* by James Kerr. It's an amazing journey of legacy through the eyes of the All Blacks, a must-read for anyone trying to build a culture, a team, or to do transformational work.)

I start every school year asking the same questions:

- What do you want our legacy to be?
- What do you want *your* legacy to be?

A sign hangs at the entrance to our school that sets my expectation for legacy. It says: *Leave Fred Lynn better than you found it!*

I believe that life is about the opportunity you have to impact the world around you; that's your legacy. I've noticed that school leaders and teachers don't talk about legacy enough. When I speak with educators and students, I ask two questions:

- What is your one word?
- What do you want your legacy to be?

The response I get most often to these two questions, no matter where I go, is blank stares . . . sometimes uncomfortable smiles. People really struggle with defining their legacy, because just like the word *love*, it's not something we talk about in school enough. My hope is that you will start to consider the legacy you want to leave and start the conversation with people around you to get them thinking as well.

Are You Willing to Work for It?

Some people talk about wanting to leave a legacy, but not everyone is willing to do the work. When your feet hit the ground each morning, you have an opportunity to make your mark. And every day, you have the chance to build on your legacy. But it isn't easy. You have to push past your comfort zone and be willing to go one more round—every day. Chasing something bigger than yourself requires work and effort. There are no shortcuts. There are no quick fixes. You can't just tweet, snap, Facebook, or *insta* your way to a legacy. You have to put in the work. But first you have to decide what your legacy will be.

So what do you want your legacy to be? What do you want to be remembered for when everything is said and done? What are people going to say about you?

Don't leave your legacy up to chance. Don't let someone else tell your story. Let your actions tell your story. Let your life speak for itself. Your legacy is your story to write. Every sacrifice, every drop of blood, sweat, tears you shed, the love you show when you stand up for the weak—those are the things that shape your legacy.

Today is the only thing we have, right now, living in the moment. Yesterday is gone, and the only guarantee about tomorrow is that you do not know what tomorrow will bring! It's important to have dreams and plans for the future, but preparation for the future should not come at the expense of living today. The reality is life is so fragile and so short. Time passes so quickly. It seems like you blink, and forty years have passed you by. We have to live in the moment, make each and every minute count. Decide today to live with passion and purpose. If you need to make a change, do it! If you have children, don't let there be any regrets; be there for them now. Instead of worrying about what other people think or say, hold yourself accountable to you and the people you love most.

Living in the moment also requires that you stop looking backward. So many people (particularly educators) get caught up living in the past, bringing up old war stories or talking about "how we've always done things." Negative conversations about people or the past will only get you down. Choose to surround yourself with amazing, like-minded people who will work and grow beside you. Remember, your future is determined by whom you hang out with because you are the average of the five people you hang out with most. We tell our students that all the time, and it's just as true for each of us.

I want you to look at yourself in the mirror each night before you go to bed and ask yourself these questions:

- Was I better for children today?
- Did I give everything I had for the people around me?

You are the only one who can answer these questions. And you are the person who has to live with yourself, your decisions, and actions.

My goal is to be able to put my head on the pillow every night knowing that I gave everything. There is nothing I wouldn't do to ensure my students have what they need to be successful. My relentless determination for my kids is followed closely by my commitment to my teachers and staff who are working with me to carry out our mission.

If you're like me, you may even have trouble sleeping at night because you can't stop thinking about your students. I am always wondering if they are safe, warm, and loved. I wonder what else I could have done that day. It's hard to turn off those thoughts because caring about kids is what I do—it's who I am. I want to be the difference in my children's and community's lives. I refuse to sit down on the sidelines and talk about change and offer solutions. In my community, I bring the hope. I am the one who is going to disrupt the norm. And I am prepared to sacrifice it all to win for my students and community.

What about you? What does your community say about you? Do you know what it will take to ensure their success? Are you willing to go that far?

What Defines You?

Jonathan Alsheimer
seventh-grade teacher

The most fearless of lions were not born in the luxury of captivity but in the ferociousness of the wild. It was there that they learned to fight and claw for every inch. The same holds true for the greatest teachers and leaders in education. Success is a choice. No one is born a great leader. The greatest leaders find a way to set themselves apart and do the toughest jobs. They don't just stand in the trenches next to you, but they stand in front of you. Hamish Brewer exemplifies all of those attributes through his leadership and ability to galvanize the people around him through one word: *relentless*. He encourages his teachers to look in the mirror and ask themselves each day, "What will your legacy be?" He challenges his students to understand that they are not defined by a letter or number.

No matter who you are, it is your determination, resilience, hard work, grit, and attitude that define you. When the world says you can't, it's what you do next that matters. Be relentless.

4

LESSONS FROM THE FIRE TRUCK

I didn't know anyone in Virginia when I moved here in 2003. I was coming off a year of backpacking and exploring the world. Moving gave me the opportunity do what I loved—teach—and to continue traveling. My first stateside teaching assignment was in Falmouth, Virginia, a suburb of Fredericksburg. Everything was new to me and felt like an adventure—including driving, which I'd never done on the right before. But after a few days of driving around in my new town, I found my bearings and a Walmart. I figured that was a successful start. I was good to go!

While out exploring one day shortly after I arrived, I noticed a sign outside the local fire station that read, "Free training. Inquire inside." It took me a few days, but I worked up the courage and went into the Company 2 station to ask about the training. I've always wanted to experience life to the fullest, and I needed some new friends. I thought this might be an interesting way to do both. *Why not?!*

The fire service of Stafford County had its own culture. It had a multigenerational history as a volunteer fire department where many local families gave their time and energy to the community. The men and women in this volunteer system lived, slept, and breathed their firehouse. From the moment I entered the doors, I was hooked! I loved the competition, camaraderie, and the adrenaline rush that came from answering the calls. There is nothing more thrilling than the rush that comes when you hear the alarms sounding, the firehouse doors rolling up, and the roar of the engine with its sirens blaring. In that moment, you know someone is counting on you to show up with your A game and be the difference—sometimes between life and death. I couldn't get enough.

I started my training at Company 2, a truck company, but moved to Company 1, a rescue company, just a few weeks later. It was closer to home—and it was the firehouse that served the community where I was teaching. I thought it made a lot of sense to be at the firehouse in my school's backyard. Plus, the fire house's motto—"Holding All the Aces"—aligned with my own vision and mission; I wanted to *be* the ace! As the first firehouse in the county, Company 1 had a long history and had a strong membership that, like me, was aggressive about taking action. *We would go in and put the fire out!*

I would spend my days teaching and then head to the firehouse in the evening. I slept there many nights—taking calls and fighting fires—and then got up and went to school the next day to teach my fifth-grade students. It was not unusual for me to come to school a little smelly from the previous night's work, but my students didn't mind. They loved hearing stories and having the other firefighters come visit. My kids felt like they were part of the team, especially when the firehouse adopted my class and gave them each their very own Company 1, Falmouth Fire Department T-shirts. Whenever they drove by the school, my firefighting buddies would hit the sirens and blast horns to let the kids know they had their backs and were watching over them.

I finished my fire department training within six months and emerged as a leader in my recruit class. I graduated with the distinction of earning top fireman—an honor the instructors voted on. That award meant the world to me; I had worked hard and did not want to let the team or instructors down. It was clear from the outset that whether you were a paid or a volunteer recruit, if you couldn't or wouldn't measure up, you would not make the cut. We all received the same training and were held to the highest standard, and rightly so. The job entailed running into burning buildings and operating under extreme conditions with the very folk who were our trainers. They were counting on us to get it right, knowing that if we didn't, it could cost someone their life.

Training consisted of pulling hoses over and over again until we had the system down by memory. Everything we did, from working with hoses and tools to getting our gear on, always came down to how efficient and effective we could be in the shortest amount of time. We would have races during training to test how quickly we could put on our gear. I was proud when I was able to get my time down to under a minute.

During training, recruits are considered a "red helmet" and are restricted to certain activities. As a red helmet, I could ride the trucks but couldn't operate fully on the fireground or go into a burning building. I could not help myself; I was always looking for a way to prove myself, a way to show the fellas I was ready. I continually pushed the limits of what I was allowed to do—sometimes suffering the wrath of the chief—but my focus and enthusiasm showed him I was up to the challenge.

As a new recruit, the one thing I wanted most was to catch a call and put out my first fire. It's a defining moment in any firefighter's career. It's when you find out if you have what it takes. It's also the moment you prove yourself to your company. When that moment came for me, I didn't want to screw it up! I wanted to show the team that I was prepared to put my training into action. I wanted to *earn* the shirt, not just wear it. I wanted my fellow firefighters to know that they could count on me, to be confident that no matter how bad the situation was, I would be standing right there answering the call, ready to put my life on the line for any one of my brothers and for the taxpaying citizens who needed our help.

When I finally got my opportunity to go on my first fire call after graduation, I kind of failed; in fact, I blew it! The alarms went off, and I jumped on the truck. We arrived on the location, and I ran to get the hoses and got ready to enter the building. I was doing everything right! I got to the front door, where smoke was pouring out, and sized up the scene. I knew the fire was in the front bedroom on the second floor, so I ran up the stairs with the hose. That's when I realized I wasn't wearing half of my gear. I was missing my Nomex (a protective hood worn under a firefighter's helmet), and my gloves weren't on right. Before I knew it, I was burning up, which is when I broke one of the two cardinal rules of our company, which are don't drop the line and don't give it up to anyone from another crew. Thankfully, I was able to give the line to one of our own, but I had to drop the line and leave the building. I reset myself and went back in, but that night I was given what for by my chief—and rightly so! I had let everyone down, and my performance had embarrassed myself and my company. Embarrassing myself was okay, but the department? Hell no!

My only saving grace that day was that I had shown that I was not afraid to go into the fire. I proved that when the alarms sounded and the bells rang and the gates to hell opened, I was ready to go into battle. That night was a long, restless one, during which it crossed my mind that it would be easier to not show my face the next day. But that's not who I am. Before I finally fell asleep, I determined to prove myself.

Less than twenty-four hours later, I got my chance. The bells sounded, the doors rolled up, and we dropped the throttle to a house on fire. This time I was ready! Instead of charging out, I took a couple extra seconds to ready myself. Air? Check! Gloves and Nomex? Check! Tools? Check! Go, go, go! Let's go!

I'll never forget that call. We beached the engine in the front yard and went to work. I grabbed the hose and ran up to the side door, where Chief was on his knees telling me to get my ass in there. I threw my air on and went into the crackling, pitch-black building. *This isn't good*, I thought. We couldn't find fire, which meant only one thing: a chance of a flashover, where everything could just burst into flames. I was grateful to have a seasoned fireman, Jimmy Kelley, on the hose with me. He told me to get down, so we crouched low as we moved forward, all the while using a stream of water from the hose to make a fog-pattern umbrella as a heat shield. Seconds later, the house erupted in fire all around us— wall to wall, floor to ceiling, and blasting through the roof. Once we saw the red stuff, it was game on! I was out to prove that I could be the best of the best! Jimmy and I fought side by side to slay the dragon, and when the time came, the crew had to drag me out—I was in the zone! When I finally came out of the building, my fire chief tackled me and shouted, "You're a fireman now! You're a real fuckin' fireman! You can ride my trucks any time!"

"We don't rise to the occasion; we fall back on our training."

Chris Smith
volunteer fire chief, DCFD, Rescue 2

When Hamish came to Falmouth, I had already been warned about this guy from New Zealand who talked funny, talked a lot, with somewhat of a storied past, and had self-proclaimed how good he was going to be at the job. That combination immediately caused me to form a negative opinion of him. Fortunately for Hamish, there were guys vouching for him whom I respected, so I decided to reserve judgment until I met him. The moment we spoke, I instantly felt his energy but gave him about a 50 percent chance of making it as a firefighter and even less to become a "Falmouth Fireman."

Once Firefighter Level 1 and 2 classes began, I was encouraged to hear that Hamish was the class leader and was excelling in the course. When he wasn't in class or working his regular job as a teacher, he was at the station perfecting his newfound craft. After a few months, I attended his graduation ceremony.

Fast forward to July 4, 2005, Independence Day. Hamish fit in nicely at Falmouth but was still a rookie with a lot to learn. Little did he know he was about to learn a hard lesson that evening. Around dinner time, Stafford Emergency Communications dispatched a town-house fire, which meant Engine 1 was due first on the scene. Hamish was assigned to the "line" that night. The line is the position that uses the nozzle to directly extinguish the fire. Engine 1 arrived on scene with smoke showing from the second floor, and I saw the crew enter the house with the hose. I happened to be the incident commander, and by all accounts, it should have been a routine fire, if there is such a thing. The next thing I saw was Hamish coming down the steps quickly yelling something about forgetting a part of his protective gear. He attempted to correct the mistake, but by that time, someone else completed his job. That minor lack of attention to detail cost him the chance to put out the fire, his first fire.

That night and the whole next day, the guys gave Hamish a hard time. He took all of it, and I could tell he was using it as fuel to ensure perfection the next time. When the building-fire tone sounded the next day, I happened to arrive first to find a single-story block building with smoke pouring out of every opening. Smoke gave me a visual clue about how violent the fire raging inside was. Engine 1, with Hamish "running the line" again, arrived next. As soon as the parking brake hit, Hamish grabbed the hose line and deployed it to the door. I watched him get completely dressed for what awaited him and his crew inside. The line was charged with water, and off they went crawling under the smoke into the now well-involved building. From my vantage point, I watched them systematically extinguish the fire. Even when I couldn't see them, I could hear Hamish. In short order, Engine 1 was relieved (reluctantly) by another company. Their job was done. Hamish had redeemed himself. I was extremely proud and remember hugging him when he came out. His persistence, work ethic, and attitude when the chips were down were the reason he succeeded. In our job, we have a saying that "We don't rise to the occasion; we fall back on our training." On July 5, 2005, Hamish did exactly that. At that moment, Hamish became a "Falmouth Fireman."

Never in my life had I felt that kind of fulfillment and belonging. I was home. I was part of a team where everyone was all-in for each other. I knew there was nothing we wouldn't do for each other and no place we wouldn't be willing to go to defend one another. In the years that have followed, I have drawn so much from that experience. When I think about the sense of belonging I want to create in my school or the kind of leader I want to be, that moment is what comes to mind every time.

Over the course of the first year in the fire service, I spent my every waking moment outside school hours at the firehouse. It was around Halloween 2005, when an accident changed my life forever. I was asleep at the firehouse when a call went out around five in the morning. As I climbed out of bed and ran down to get on the fire truck, one of my fireman brothers, Michael Anthenry, asked me if I wanted him to go on the run so that I could get to school on time. "I got one more. No worries, mate," I assured him.

We were responding to a 911 call; it was a CPR in progress that got upgraded to a cardiac arrest. We were driving through the area, and I noticed from the front seat where I was riding as the officer that there were a lot of S curves. When we came around the corner on Plantation Drive, the truck leaned past the point of no return, and we then began to roll. We rolled until the truck finally came to a stop on its side. To this day, I still do not know how I ended up outside the fire truck. Looking around, I saw a massive radius of debris that had come from the brand-new fire truck that was now destroyed!

I do not remember much from those first moments after the accident, but I do recall lying on the ground waiting for help to come and seeing a great light. I heard someone ask, "Are you ready to go?" I vividly remember saying, "I'm not ready." In the next moment, I saw my fire department friends around me trying to help put me on a stretcher to medevac me by helicopter to the hospital. I had never been so scared. It felt as if my life had just flashed right in front of me. In all the chaos of that morning, everything felt so silent and cold. I did a quick assessment of myself as I lay there: *Do my toes move? Do my fingers move?* I thought I was okay, but I couldn't feel anything in my back. The back felt locked, and since I was strapped onto the stretcher, I couldn't move anyway. My fire chief came to check on me just before they loaded me onto the helicopter, and even with everyone around me, I felt alone and frightened. I was this indestructible, kick-ass fireman. I wanted to save the world. And there I lay unable to move at all.

As it had turned out, my back was broken. The doctors told me I should have been dead or paralyzed given what they could see on the X-rays. During the first few weeks after the accident, I knew something wasn't right. Doctors kept telling me I'd be okay and that I would heal, but my body, balance, and feeling of my back slipping left me feeling not convinced, so I kept asking for second and third opinions. I finally found Dr. Squillante, a confident man who didn't flinch when it was time to decide.

He quickly ascertained what we needed to do. He assured me that, with surgery, I could get better. He put six pins in my back, after first thinking I was going to need only three pins, and after about three months of bed rest, I started rehabilitation.

It took a year to get my muscles strong enough and to relearn how to walk without an aid or having to sit down for a rest. I had to wear a back brace to keep my back stabilized. And I had to do the work, every day. While working in the pool or gym at the rehabilitation center, I knew it was up to me—and no one else—to do whatever it took to get better. My goal was to be able to get back on the fire truck, but I had to start by getting my muscles strong enough to stand, walk, and then finally—hopefully—able to run.

Even though my recovery was difficult, I felt as if I had gotten a second chance at life. I know I've been given a second chance to be the difference for others—and I don't ever take that for granted! During recovery, my girlfriend at the time, Ashley Dowling, never left my side. That's when I knew I had met my future wife. (We got married and now have four amazing children together.) I know that every day that I'm alive is an opportunity to live with passion and purpose—to relentlessly live life to the fullest!

LESSONS FROM THE FIRE SERVICE THAT APPLY TO EDUCATION

I have applied so many lessons and principles from my experience as a firefighter to life as an educator and leader. For example, I wanted to be the best on the team so that the people working with me could trust me with their lives. Within my school, I want my teachers to feel like they are the best in the business. We talk about teaching on fire, which means that they can and should be aggressive about being the answer for our students and community. Another principle is that of preparation. In education, the great teachers are the ones who know the curriculum, know their students, and are prepared for a meaningful day of instruction. In the fire service, preparation was essential. We spent so much time repeating the simplest of exercises because it's the little things done well that add up to great accomplishments. Winning is not about one big play; it's about doing the little things well, consistently, and effectively.

Every day that I'm alive is an opportunity to live with passion and purpose—to relentlessly live life to the fullest!

Others First—Always

Kevin Good
assistant fire chief, Fort Belvoir
volunteer fire chief, Stafford County

My first encounter with Hamish was at the Falmouth Volunteer Firehouse, around 2003, where he was leaning up against the back of one of the rigs telling stories with a group of dedicated volunteer firefighters. I was an assistant chief at the time in Stafford County, Virginia's busiest firehouse. I had just returned from a weeknight meeting, where I quietly joined the crowd to hear this fella, who was covered in tattoos, talking with others like he had been a member forever. I wondered who in the heck this guy was. I thought, *I hope this is a good dude, but man, he speaks out.* Time rolled on, and I got to know this guy Hamish and quickly learned he was one to speak his mind and not be intimidated by anything or anyone.

Fast forward to the morning of November 1, 2005, when I was notified that that our fire truck had been involved in a rollover accident with three of my firefighters injured. "Are they okay, and who was on the truck?" I asked. My immediate focus was on the firefighters and helping them recover physically and mentally from the tragic event. All the men were hurt, and it was well known that Hamish was expected to suffer the longest road of all. I knew he would never be the same; his life had changed.

Firefighters always try to make others feel better, and his situation was no different. I visited him in the hospital and talked with him, but I was scared that he had been ruined by just one accident. In our conversations, my intention was to have him not worry about his career. He would always respond with, "I'm good, bro." One afternoon as I got ready to leave his hospital room, he asked me for a favor. "I need you to pick up some flowers and take them to Ashley," he said. She was his girlfriend at the time and had returned from college after the accident to be by his side.

Hamish had already shown me he wasn't average. No matter how bad he hurt, he would find a way to get what he wanted! He taught me that you can achieve anything regardless of your situation. In the coming days, I met his Falmouth Elementary School principal, Gayle Thyring, to figure out his leave and pay issues. All Hamish wanted to know was how he could get time off for Ashley's college graduation that coming spring. We didn't know, with his back injuries, what life would physically be like for Hamish, but he wasn't worried about that. He was determined to be at Ashley's graduation no matter what because he wanted her to know how special she was to him. I didn't want him to travel, but he wanted what he wanted, and there was no convincing him of something different.

Little did I know that an accident I wasn't personally involved in would change my life forever. Through this journey and a lifetime friendship with this "off the chain" leader, I've realized that life isn't about me. It's about the impact I can make on others. Hamish's resilience to his tragic situation influenced me to focus on others. It also taught me that a never-give-up attitude, grit, and top-shelf determination are contagious.

Here are more lessons from the fire truck:

1. Teamwork and Camaraderie

There is nothing more important than the team. No one person should cast a shadow over the team; no one person is more important than another. Your team is the product of its weakest link, which means everyone has the responsibility to be his or her best—and empower others do the same. It's ride or die. The only question is *whose car are we taking?*

One of the sayings at my school is, "When you look over your shoulder, who will be standing there?"

The answer is simple: "Every single one of us!" We are in this together! When you're choosing your team, surround yourself with like-minded people who want to win championships and change the outcomes of not just schools but entire communities. Look for people who will put it all on the line to be the difference for your students and one another.

2. Accountability and Attention to Details

In the fire service, success comes down to attention to detail: the way you check out the engine and equipment at the beginning of each shift, clean the firehouse, or practice the most boring of exercises, pulling hoses. The same is true in schools. It's easier to put off planning, to not want to fully participate in a professional learning community (PLC), or to close your door and just worry about your own results. That's for average schools and average educators.

Determine to build a culture where everyone is willing to go the extra mile and take care of the details during planning and preparation. Be *on fire* for instruction. I have never met a teacher who can be outstanding in the classroom without first learning the curriculum, preparing well, and taking pride in his or her craft. Success just doesn't come that way. Hard work, attention to detail, and intentional effort will always carry the day and ensure that your school experiences success.

3. Leadership

Any leader worth following is a leader who leads by example and is willing to do the work. There is no place for egos on the fire truck or in the schoolhouse. Everyone's input is valued. Everyone's efforts and actions determine the outcome. How you lead—regardless of your title—can mean the difference between success and failure.

4. Decision-Making

Great leadership is about being able to listen to and empower those around you. When you are in the middle of an emergency on the fireground, each person needs to be able to make snap decisions and deliver on their job responsibilities—without anyone else telling them which moves to make. Similar to a fire scene, classroom scenarios can change rapidly. Teachers must be able to adapt to whatever conditions come their way. They need to feel empowered to make decisions in the moment—without having to ask for permission or wait for approval. If you are in leadership, empower your teachers to make decisions without you. You cannot be there 100 percent of the time, and if your people have to wait on you for a decision, then *you* become a barrier in the instructional process, stymieing creativity and risk-taking and ultimately preventing your educators from being the best they can be for children.

5. Pride

Firemen take great pride in their firehouse, from what it stands for, down to the way the rigs and engine bay floors get washed. In Company 1, we took great pride in our message, vision, and attention to detail, and how we responded in the most extreme conditions. In the same way, we should take pride in our classrooms, our schools, and in our performance. We should want to be the very best at all times, ready to perform when we are most needed. Never forget we take care of the most valuable resource in our school and a parent's most prized possession.

5

THINK OPPORTUNITY, NOT OBLIGATION

On any given day, the students in your class could be just like I was as a kid—in desperate need of help and love, wanting to feel appreciated and heard. Being a student was difficult for me; in fact, it still is. I have shared some of my story in these pages, and just like me, our students have stories to tell. Some of their stories are more difficult and heart-wrenching than others, ranging from families chasing the American dream of freedom and prosperity to students just trying to find love and acceptance at something . . . anything. In today's school rooms, there are students whose families have been torn apart because of divorce, drugs, domestic violence, and neglect. There are horror stories of loss due to wars, gangs, corruption, and violence. One time a student shared with me (through Google Translate) that he had witnessed the death of family members to senseless violence. He told me about how he had traveled many days and nights, overcoming multiple hardships in his journey to the United States.

My students serve as a constant reminder of the magnitude and the meaning of the work we do each and every day as educators. Their stories keep me grounded; their struggles and successes help me to stay humble and be thankful for what I have. They also help me to remember as Dr. Eric Johnson has spoken on, it is impossible to serve others well if we think we are better than them.

You can't serve someone you think you are better than!

The world around us may not always believe in or appreciate the individual students in our schools, but we *must*. We must believe in their ability to learn and to succeed in life. Regardless of their stories or their circumstances, we have to remember that students are not failures or broken beyond repair. Our job is to not just teach them the academic information they need to succeed in life but also, and most importantly, the character traits they need in order to thrive in life. We need to empower them to believe in themselves and in their ability to do anything they set out to accomplish. Speaking for myself, I want every kid I come into contact with to know that I believe in them and that I will never give up on them. Anything less than the kind of commitment that says, "I'd go through a brick wall and back for you," is unacceptable.

You can't serve someone you think you are better than!

TEACH THEM TO DREAM—AND PLAN

Just like each of our students is unique, each of their journeys and dreams will be different. The way we reach them and teach them should be different too. If you consider how little schools have really changed in comparison to how the world and technology have changed around us, we have a ton of opportunity to improve the way we teach and how our classrooms look and operate! Aside from updating day-to-day teaching practices and moving away from compliance-based classes where students sit in nice, neat rows, the way we think about what's best for students' futures needs to be updated as well. We shouldn't assume that every kid will travel the same path, nor should we expect that every child will want—or need—to go to college. Yes, I would love to see every single child continue their education beyond high school, but the fact of the matter is that college isn't for everyone. We have to acknowledge that it is okay for students to pick different paths; for example, many students can have purposeful and lucrative careers in the fields of trade. All over the country today, thousands of trade jobs are waiting to be filled without a ready workforce for them. My point is that rather than pushing students along the career and education lines of what we think is appropriate for them, let's talk with them about their dreams for the future and their current goals.

Whatever the starting point or the end destination, we need to encourage our students to follow their ideas, dreams, and aspirations; however, we can't stop at dreaming. It's the dreams with plans behind them that have the best chance for success. We should engage our students through the skill sets and interests that have captured their imagination; for example, students love being entrepreneurs. That was true when I was a kid and the focus was on trading sports cards or mowing lawns, but today's students up the ante by starting their own businesses online. They are young, up-and-coming entrepreneurs. If teens can be successful, as one of my former students was, in selling used shoes online, imagine what could happen if we challenged our students to excel as entrepreneurs and tapped into their interests through the instruction in our classrooms?

One more thought about looking to the future: I understand that we want our students to be successful in the next grade or school, but the conversation around preparing kids for the next year drives me crazy. If we spent as much time and energy teaching in the moment as we do on preparing students for the next year, or for middle school, or high school, or college, then we would be a formidable force of laser focus and execution of opportunity for our students. The way we best prepare our students for their future is by focusing on their individual needs in *this* moment. It's so easy to make the mistake of getting ahead of ourselves in life and forgetting to be present in the very thing or person standing in front of us. Let's teach our students to give 100 percent *now* wherever they are.

From One of the Toughest Schools to One of the Best

Teanna
eighth-grade student

I moved to Woodbridge, Virginia, when I was seven. In all honesty, I wasn't excited about it. Little did I know what my new school, Occoquan Elementary, had in store for me. I met my new principal, Mr. Brewer. In my head, I thought he was just a normal principal. I was wrong. The four years that I went to Occoquan were entirely different than any other school I had attended previously. Mr. Brewer brought tribes to the school, had pep rallies and parties, painted our plain white walls, and interacted with us, unlike other principals. In addition, and most importantly, he showed us love and taught us valuable lessons that we didn't even realize would help us later in life. He gave my peers and me a reason to want to go to school and learn.

Elementary school came to an end, and it was finally time to go off to middle school. I was zoned for Fred Lynn Middle. There was not one person who didn't seem to talk negatively about it. My first year in middle school was up and down, which made my experience not quite the one I imagined.

The following year, Mr. Brewer became the new principal at Fred Lynn. Within the first few weeks, there were already dramatic changes. Grades and test scores improved, staff members were enthusiastic, and the school discipline completely changed around. Our school went from one of the worst-rated schools to one of the best. We were even accredited for the first time in years.

I think I speak for everyone that Mr. Brewer has worked with when I say that he has impacted our lives. He inspires us to "chase

100," be our best selves, and not put ourselves in bad situations. Mr. Brewer looks out for his students and staff and makes sure they know he loves and cares for them. Every day, he tells us, "If somebody didn't tell you today that they love you, Mr. Brewer is telling you he loves you." It's truly amazing, and I'm proud to call him my family.

TEAR OFF THE LABELS

People ask me all the time how our school reaches such a broad range of student groups; for example, how we help special education (SPED) and English for speakers of other language (ESOL) students reach such great heights. The answer lies in the question itself. Our students are not labels. They are not numbers. They are not defined by a test score or letter grade. Our students—all of our students—are the most important resource in our buildings; school is not school without them.

Students today are ready, able, and wanting to learn more so than ever before. I have never met a student who can't learn, and if a teacher comes to me and says, "This student can't learn," then I know that teacher has given up on the student. We can't give up! We've got to work on ways to reach students differently—focusing on their needs, rather than sticking to our methods.

While I believe that every single student can, I also know that every student's journey is different. It will take students different lengths of time and pathways to reach their goals and destinations. But we've got to be careful about applying labels to students and about how we meet their different needs. Don't let labels limit our kids! Take students with special or different needs, for example. While there is certainly a time and place for small group, pull-out

Our students—all of our students— are the most important resource in our buildings; school is not school without them.

instruction, that does not mean we should put students who have disabilities or challenges on an island. They do not learn from being separated from their peers all the time; in fact, when they are pulled from their classrooms, they often miss out on huge chunks of curriculum. We should instruct and teach our students' deficits through the curriculum, not through the disability. All too often, we make the mistake of teaching to just the disability or the skill deficit without teaching curriculum. If we reverse that cycle and teach the disability or deficit *through* the curriculum, we accomplish two goals at once. The scary thing is, when we only teach to the students' deficit, they can go long periods of time without working on their curriculum. Then we wonder why they're struggling with the material.

Students know and feel when they are being treated differently. Getting pulled from class often leaves them feeling embarrassed and bad about themselves and their schooling. Their self-esteem and confidence take a hit every time. It's our duty, as educators, to build up our students and instill in them the confidence and habits that will empower them to achieve anything they set their minds to. We must teach them how to fail forward, get back up, and go one more round.

CHASING 100 AND OTHER IDEAS FOR TEACHING DIFFERENTLY

Earlier in this chapter, I touched on the idea that we need to do things differently and to think in new ways about education. Some of the changes that make a huge impact are small and subtle. Others completely alter the way the individual classroom and the school as a whole operates. One of the more subtle changes I've incorporated through the years is the idea of *chasing 100*.

Empowering Belief

Catherine Waller
one of Hamish's first students in New Zealand
actor/writer/producer

Hamish Brewer was my teacher in New Zealand in my final two years of elementary school. What always struck me was the impact he had on our entire school with his huge heart, bold methods of listening to his students, and demand for us to be our truest selves. He created a safe space for each of us to *be*. *He* celebrated our diverse needs, desires, hopes, and dreams for our future. He really knew us, and he stood fiercely for us and always empowered us and listened for our greatness. And he celebrated the end of each term with the best class party a ten-year-old could ask for.

Mr. Brewer listened to me at ten years old—when I didn't even know I needed someone to talk to. I would have kept it in, but he allowed me to cry. That kind of freedom of self-expression is what empowered me to pursue my artistic ventures. I am now a performing artist in New York City. When I saw a video of Mr. Brewer on Facebook, I tracked him down and thanked him for being my teacher. It was amazing to be able to tell him that I am living the life of my dreams.

Mr. Brewer's commitment to young people makes a difference far beyond one school year, and well beyond a grade. Thank you, Mr. Brewer, for who you are. You may never know the difference you have made, and will continue to make, for people around the world.

When we box students into a test score or letter grade, we fail them, particularly if we demand perfection. Asking students to get a perfect score robs them of their courage to take risks, explore, and try new things. You already know that I want my students (and staff, and myself, for that matter) to give their best. But rather than make an unrealistic demand for perfection, I ask my students to "chase 100" every day. I know that if they are chasing 100, then they are striving to give their very best each and every day. That is a subtle difference in wording. The impact is huge. Students begin to change their mindsets from focusing on getting a perfect test score or letter grade to focusing on own their learning and on an attitude of learning and performing to the best of their ability.

In an earlier chapter, I mentioned the sign that hung in my room when I was a young teacher: "Pride in Performance." That message applies here as well. We can start by challenging students to take pride in their effort and in themselves. Then, once they know what it means to take pride in themselves as individuals, we can explore what it means to take pride in their class and in their school. When we tap into our students' best efforts, then pride, motivation, and inspiration become infectious. The momentum of goodwill and positive action becomes a movement that transforms your school's entire culture.

Social Media and Smartphones

Technology has changed what a classroom and schoolhouse should look and feel like. If you think about it, though, the Apple iPhone was released in 2007. It feels like it has been around forever, when it truly has only been in existence for just over a decade. It took several years for smartphones to be commonly used by adults, and only recently have smartphones become the center of debates about whether they are "a must-have device" for students in our schools.

Smartphone technology has changed so much of our day-to-day life. Consider the power of social media and the various apps used for communication, such as Instagram and Snapchat. I believe that many of our students' challenges, academically and socially, stem from social media "communication." In reality, relying on social media has led to breakdowns in communication between students, parents, and teachers, and it encourages behavior that is not entirely honest.

Case in point: Snapchat. I hate Snapchat. I hate the fact students can send an image that disappears after it's opened. I can't help but notice how many students' personal, emotional, and relational challenges right now originate on Snapchat. Groups and individuals bully others by posting photos and negative messages about them. This seems to get worse when school is out of session. During the holiday break, students communicate with one another through social media—and often do and say things they wouldn't in real life. Upon returning to school from the break, students have to face their demons in real life, often with regret. It's not that the kids themselves are bad, but they don't have the maturity or experience to know how to bail out of bad interactions. And they end up getting in too deep—and into trouble.

I tell the students every day, "Delete Snapchat. Nothing good ever comes of it." The students crack up when I tell them this. When Snapchat went down for an afternoon one weekend, someone started a rumor I was somehow able to interrupt the service. Come Monday morning, when the students began investigating my influence in the event, I did not confirm or deny my involvement. For a solid day, the word was that I had brought down Snapchat. It wasn't true, obviously, but it was fun to imagine.

The implications of phone use in schools goes beyond social media. How often do students pull out their phones to take a video? This is fine until it isn't. The students who record fights or bullying disturb me more sometimes than those who are the center of it. Once a phone goes up and the camera is on, the students who are actually in the confrontation often do not know how to back down. They feel they have to do *something* or risk being labeled weak or a coward. Without a video camera egging them on, or the crowd for that matter, the reality is that students will often attempt to talk their way out of a fight.

Before you say that I'm sending schools back to the Dark Ages, I want to say that I do see the value and essential need for technology in schools. Schools, classrooms, and instruction need to look, sound, and feel different than ever before. Technology has opened amazing doors! It's because of technology and even social media platforms that our students today understand concepts of ownership, collaboration, and communication—earlier than any generation before them. These tools empower our students to feel and own their individualism. So, even as we call upon strategies and ideas that have stood the test of time, we must engage our students in ways that enable them to express their individuality to the world.

Student Discipline

While we're talking about attitudes and practices that need to change, let's address student discipline. Student discipline has long been a challenge in schools, none more so than in Title I schools like mine where often students are not concerned about consequences. In many cases, they challenge us to send them home so that they can get some uninterrupted, unchaperoned time off to go play Fortnite.

I have said it before and will say it again: Unless the actions are egregious and harmful to others, suspending students does not work. If it worked, we wouldn't have any problems, right?

Suspending students from school is like taking medication for a toothache. The cause for the toothache doesn't go away; the medication just masks the pain temporarily.

If school policy is to simply send kids home rather than to deal with the situation, those kids may well end up in a pipeline to prison. I am not talking about the outliers who do something appalling. I'm talking about the hundreds of students who are suspended every day for infractions of archaic rules and policies, none of which, when broken, hurt or even affect others. I will *never* allow a student to inhibit another student's learning due to disruptive behavior. Let's be clear on that. But it should be okay for a student to make a mistake. When school is a place to learn from mistakes and grow as a result, we then begin to serve our real mission: to prepare students to live a purposeful and intentional life.

An effective discipline strategy I employ is working with students through their mistakes. My students know that I am as hard as nails. They also know that I love them. Because we share mutual respect built on meaningful relationships, they are willing to talk, listen, and learn.

In my first year of teaching, I learned not to back students into the corner when it comes to discipline issues. When you wage war with students, everyone loses. When you back students into the corner and give them no way out, all they know how to do is fight back to save face, especially if their peers are watching. Unfortunately, this happens all the time in schools. An adult tries to hold a student accountable without ensuring that student maintains his or her dignity—and the situation either escalates or the student shuts down and loses all respect for the adult.

Discipline is not about being out to *get* students; it's about being out to *help* students. That's why I always remind the students who come to me for discipline issues, "I don't like what you did, but I still love you." I make sure they know that I respect their honesty. And before our conversation is over, I ask, "Was I fair today?" Never forget that the way we treat students ensures a mutual response—for good or bad.

The non-suspension consequences I have used over the years have been a little *alternative*, but they are effective. I always discuss my alternative plan of action with parents, and they are always on board. Parents know that any consequences are assigned with the right heart because they know I care about their children. When it's not winter, I love assigning school projects outside, from cleaning spaces to gardening and fixing things. It's a sort of school service during which the students' sense of belonging and community grows. They gain a feeling of pride when they can see the fruits of their labor; it feels good. Sometimes I have students help the custodians with their work for a period of time. They clean up the school, take out the trash, and in the process, they feel as if they are contributing and giving back. It's not unusual for students to ask if their friends can join in and help them.

Think about the projects you may have coming up, such as a mural or book room. In both of these examples, our school saved money by having the students help us with the preparation; for example, painting the base coat of the mural. The students had a blast doing this and took pride in knowing they were helping bring a project to life. I've found that students love taking ownership in their school. When they participate in projects around the school and give back, a sense of community develops that can impact them and the school in other positive ways. One example from my school occurred when students designed and painted their own messages and murals. They especially took ownership of this in the bathrooms and transformed those spaces in our school.

More often than not, these suspension-alternative assignments have helped my students learn from their mistakes. They have been able to move forward (rather than become resentful) because they were treated fairly with respect and experienced a new sense of ownership, community, and pride!

An Alternative Approach to Discipline through Community

A few years ago, we started a community partnership with a local business, Occoquan Bay Fitness in Woodbridge, Virginia. The owner of the organization is Nick Mann, a retired United States Marine Corps officer and instructor. Mann led one of our staff meetings on teamwork, health, and well-being, which spurred our catch phrase, "Protect the wall, protect the hive." (Our school's mascot is the hornet.) Further conversations with him led to questions about ways we could help students, particularly those who are having discipline issues at school. We came up with a plan to start an after-school club that was focused on discipline, health, and well-being, and so our after-school CrossFit program was born. We opened the program up to all our students. Those students who were facing a suspension got to participate in the Boot Camp CrossFit program.

Our students loved the program, and so did their parents. I find that parents love that throwback to some old-fashioned values of hard work, sweat, and tough love. It's not old, and it's not new. It just works, and we all can relate to it.

The upshot of this program is that we are now developing a gym in our school that is as good as any fitness center you would pay to go to. Every single student receives a plan for fitness and health that is monitored and assessed throughout the year. Additionally, our physical education program provides instruction in strength and conditioning, health and nutrition, skills performance, and movement. The students' performance in the CrossFit program has led to improved performance in the classroom and in discipline. Most importantly, it has set up all of our students for long-term success by leading healthier lifestyles.

Seek and Teach Responsibility

Nick Mann

founder and executive director, Strength2Change

It has been an honor and pleasure to collaborate with Mr. Hamish Brewer as a community partner. Together we have created an after-school program for students and an online fitness program for faculty, both of which focus on instilling the principles of health, wellness, and fitness. With the student program alone, we have been able to reach more than two hundred students and average thirty-five to fifty student-participants each day. Mr. Brewer's support of and dedication to our programs and partnership have been unwavering.

Through our partnership, Mr. Brewer has demonstrated his ability to think outside the box, innovate, and take risks to provide the highest level of educational experience for his students. This is an uncommon trait among many of today's educational leaders, who would prefer to play it safe and only meet the status quo. I immediately saw this in person as I visited and met with countless principals who couldn't find the time in their day to build outside relationships to benefit their students and staff in a way that transcends education through lifelong health and wellness.

Mr. Brewer's mission is changing the lives of all of those he comes into contact with, no matter the challenge, no matter the work required, and no matter what others might think.

As a former Marine Corps infantry officer and leadership instructor, I want to close with a few of the Marine Corps Leadership Principles that I truly believe Mr. Hamish Brewer embodies and through which he has impacted so many:

- Know your people and look out for their welfare.
- Know yourself and seek self-improvement.
- Set the example.

- Train your unit as a team.
- Develop a sense of responsibility among your subordinates.
- Seek and take responsibility.

When it comes to school discipline, the problem in many cases is that we are reactionary rather than proactive in our approach. Students actually enjoy and thrive under structure and accountability. I am not talking about accountability based around the rules that have been invented by an adult removed from students' lives. I'm talking about the expectations that all stakeholders are invested in and follow through on every day—not just some of the time or when it suits an adult. By proactively setting and modeling expectations, holding ourselves and our students accountable, and rooting everything in our relationship with the students, we can minimize the need for discipline in schools.

A direct correlation exists between relationships, engagement, and instruction—all of which we can control as educators. Our students respond to and respect adults who engage and respect them back. They can tell when an adult does not care about them or is disinterested even in their own work. What I love about students is that they will call you out when you shortchange them. Student behavior is feedback on your relationship, preparation, effort, and instruction. As adults, we don't always want to hear that feedback, but we must not ignore it.

Trauma

Students today are faced with incredibly difficult challenges and obstacles. They are growing up around external forces that they have less control over than ever before. They are living in and around more poverty than ever before. Family units have changed; more students today live in a single-parent family. Parents work multiple jobs, and students go home to empty houses where they are forced to fend for themselves.

Hardship and trauma do not discriminate against color, religion, or zip code. Even in our more affluent schooling environments, students live in challenging circumstances. These students often struggle with bullying and drugs more so than ever before, and they are crying out for help.

I recently led our school and community through one of the hardest and most tragic student events that I have ever been through. A student from our school committed suicide. It is still something I cannot fully comprehend, and not a day that goes by where I do not think about that student. I would give it all up today to have one more opportunity to speak with this student, to do something differently—to be the difference for that child. Unfortunately, I will never get that chance. The opportunity I do have is to advocate for every single student and continue to bring and call attention to the growing problem of student suicide and trauma.

I regularly challenge educators to talk with students they don't already know well—the quiet one, the student who has different interests or doesn't seem to fit in. Every single student deserves to have an adult who cares about them, stands up for them, and is someone whom they feel they can safely reach out to. Remember this: Often that quiet child thinks of you as a hero, and you don't even know it because they are too shy to say something, or the

There are no guarantees for tomorrow in life, so live with no regrets!

student hasn't had the opportunity to communicate with you in a meaningful way. Go out every day and find one student in your building to say a quick "hello" to. Let them know you care for and love them. Ask them about themselves. You won't regret it. Some of my favorite and most inspiring conversations have come from these encounters. Plus, you never know when a conversation with a student will be your last. There are no guarantees for tomorrow in life, so live with no regrets!

RELATIONSHIPS

If you take away only one thing from this chapter, it should be this: Relationships are the most important component in engaging, inspiring, and motivating our students. Nothing else matters! Think back to the classrooms in which you personally enjoyed and learned the most. I'm willing to bet that you loved the teacher, and the teacher loved you! You had a relationship with the teacher built on respect, trust, honesty, accountability, and fun. We know the importance of relationships; this is not a new line of thinking. The trouble is, we continue to get this so wrong in education today. When I work with students who are struggling with their learning, I find the root cause is often the missing ingredient of a relationship. As adults, we have to be the bigger person in this conversation. We have to leave our egos at the door and ensure our spaces and teaching practices are not designed around the adult but designed around the students, with positive relationships at the center.

All children are opportunities—for greatness, for purpose. They are sponges ready to soak up the love, inspiration, and hope we can offer. They are thirsty for knowledge and learning, and it's up to us as educators to respond to those needs. Way too often, however, rather being seen as opportunities, children are viewed

We need to make our students' mental health and well-being a greater priority than their test scores.

as obligations. When that happens, those children are relegated to average, defeat, or failure.

You don't get to pick and choose children you will teach today. You don't get to decide who comes through the door. You can't know who will succeed and who will not. I've heard far too many times from adults that "This student has no chance in my accelerated class," or "I can't connect with that child," or "That child won't listen!" "Those children." Even worse is when I hear teachers identifying which child they think will end up in prison. It's not our job to strike the gavel and predetermine a child's outcome! Our job, our mission, our legacy is to advocate for every single one of them and ensure that all children have the opportunity to succeed in fulfilling their goals and dreams.

Our students deserve our best—every day. We must not accept excuses from ourselves or others for giving anything less. Business leaders and sports coaches often say they don't ask anything from their employees or athletes that they wouldn't give or do themselves. As educators, do we hold ourselves accountable to that same standard? Do you model the expectation of excellence for students?

As adults, our future is already in motion. Our students, however, still have the opportunity to take on the world. They will be tasked with a great responsibility and burden of straightening out the global crises that the generations before them have contributed to: pollution, climate change, disease, and food shortages. We are relying on our children and the education that they receive to ensure that, for generations to come, we live in a world of peace that is driven by people who have the ability to love, communicate, and collaborate. Our students are the opportunity for a better future!

"More Than a Principal"

Osmar
eighth-grade student

Mr. Brewer comes to students in a positive way. He motivates me to wake up and keep going with my studies. His presence makes me feel like I can do anything. When we meet in the morning or throughout the day, I know that Mr. Brewer is more than a principal; he is a friend.

Through dialogue in positive and negative situations, Mr. Brewer comforts and comes to my aid. I know that he has provided me opportunities when I was not deserving, but Mr. Brewer sees the good in me and has given me a second chance at life.

Mr. Brewer encourages team spirit through his pep rallies, random grade-level assemblies, and funny school gear that he might wear. Mr. Brewer is not afraid to put himself out there. He makes me feel free to do me and not let other people affect me. His spirit flows through all of the connections at our school.

6

TEACHING

Teaching was not my first choice for my career. I tried to leave school and join the military at the age of sixteen. At the time, students in New Zealand could finish school at sixteen, but the military didn't accept applicants that young, so that didn't work out. Next, I investigated becoming a builder. My first day on the job, the boss wanted me to dig a trench. It was the middle of summer, and the ground was rock hard. When the boss came a few hours into the day and saw that I had made no headway, we had a not-so polite discussion during which I handed him the shovel and told him to dig the hole himself. Needless to say, after walking off the job on my first day, I did not receive my paycheck. Then I decided I was going to change the world of tourism and get into the travel business. When I realized this meant sitting behind a desk and *not* traveling on planes or trains and visiting luxurious beaches around the world, I determined tourism wasn't the life for me. Then I considered becoming a physiotherapist. My interest soon faded when I learned I could not pronounce or remember the names for every muscle and bone in the body, plus it would have required a lot of hours studying which, at the time, was not my forte.

One day, my high school guidance counselor sat me down and said, "Hamish, you can't stay at school forever. You have to leave." I was seventeen years old and truly in need of some direction on finding a potential career pathway. Little did she know that I would take a path that would keep me in school forever. As we sat there eyeballing one another considering my future, a fax that she had been waiting for came through. I inquired as to what it was. She told me it was an application to "teachers college." Instantly, I responded, "I would like to go to teachers college and become a teacher."

She looked at me in surprise and said, "You're not academic enough."

"Sign me up right now," I said defiantly.

That moment was my breaking point. I was already frustrated because I didn't know what the hell I was going to do with my life. And being told I wasn't "academic enough" to succeed, well, that seemed like a dare that I had to accept. (In truth, her surprise wasn't unfounded. I never, ever gave anyone at school any reason to believe in my academic prowess.)

I filled out the paperwork and completed the essays for the teachers college application, and it hit me that I needed to start taking life a little more seriously. I couldn't go through life

I was seventeen years old and truly in need of some direction on finding a potential career pathway. Little did she know that I would take a path that would keep me in school forever.

expecting a handout. Auckland College of Education responded to my application, to my surprise, with a next-step acceptance to an interview. I couldn't believe it. It was the first time in my life that I had experienced a win when it came to an application and something academic.

On the day of the interview, I prepared by getting dressed in my "number ones," which was our school dress uniform complete with a blazer. My thought was that if I looked good for the interview, maybe my confidence would make up for what I lacked for in academics. I believed that I had a shot if I appeared confident and relied on what I saw as my most valuable skill: my ability to communicate with anyone. (What was true then is true now. The number-one skill any student needs in order to be successful is the ability to communicate well.)

I completed the interview with what I felt like were flying colors—even with a couple of doozies for answers. A few days later, I learned that I had been accepted to teachers college. *Boom*! I was on my way! My high school was not happy that I was leaving early midway through a school year because I was Deputy Head Boy— an awesome position that I had been elected for because of my commitment to all aspects of school and student body. While I struggled academically, I loved the social side of school. I knew I would miss my friends, but as I explained to them, I had to take my chances. There was no guarantee that I would be accepted to the college at a later date. To this day, I swear that the only reason I was accepted was the fact that I was a male and there was a shortage of male teachers in education.

Acceptance into Auckland College of Education, Teachers College, also meant I got accepted into The University of Auckland as part of the dual-degree and diploma program. The next four years were a true test of my perseverance, patience, and ability to finally succeed at school. I failed my first semester of college—and

What was true then is true now. The number-one skill any student needs in order to be successful is the ability to communicate well.

in one class, I learned the word *plagiarism* (even though I couldn't pronounce it). It was a hard lesson but one that would steer me right for life. A lecturer gave us an assignment to write a short-story picture book to read to children. He showed us an example and said, "Take this and copy it." Well, my level of understanding at that point was obviously not very high, so I took him at his word—literally—and handed in that book copied practically word for word and picture for picture. When I was called to task on the assignment, the lecturer soon realized I had no idea what my mistake was. Fortunately for me, the professor didn't kick me out of school. Instead, he sat me down and gave me the what for! I am not sure whether it was that conversation and my advisor's corrective action plan, or the reality that I was in danger of failing out of school, but finally something clicked for me. Suddenly the beast was awoken within me! I determined right then that I would never again fail another class, paper, or exam.

College turned out be a blast. I had found my calling. Teaching came naturally for me. I loved being around kids and soon realized the power I had to change the world through them. Teaching was what I had been searching for, waiting for, and dreaming of—I just hadn't realized it. I had dreamed, for years, of doing something big. This was it! Even so, I had no idea at the time where teaching would take me.

Being on location and assignment at schools was the most amazing experience. I had great mentors along the way who would become lifelong friends and supporters, none more so than Diane Raynes, Philip Waller, and Tracy Taylor. These mentors quickly had me figured out. They knew that I had the potential to do something special, but they saw that I was a diamond in the rough—I needed a lot of smoothing out! Boy, did these expert teachers hold me accountable with constructive feedback and nurturing support. Anyone who tells you they "love constructive feedback" is full of it. No one enjoys having their flaws and mistakes pointed out. But I learned to accept my instructors' wisdom and use it to improve. (I still didn't like it!)

I am thankful for those four years at Auckland University. The access and quality of instruction from our professors was second to none. My education prepared me through instruction and teaching practicum placements, although it wasn't until I started teaching that I truly appreciated my training. We were doing backward design and PLC planning practices before they even became a thing. I learned early on that being an amazing teacher required hard work and deep knowledge. One of the benefits, I believe, of being a New Zealand-trained teacher was that I got to teach *everything*—music, art, physical education—alongside all the core subjects of math and reading. As a fifth-grade teacher in New Zealand, I was in the pool in the summer at nine a.m. teaching kids how to swim. (We also spent a lot of time figuring out how to make a tidal wave in the pool, much to the disgust of the caretakers and principal, who would have to keep filling the pool back up with water!)

Upon graduation, I decided to take some time off and meet my partner in crime and best friend, Phil Hewitt, in England, where we would travel and work with athletes. I had worked my way through college as a fitness instructor and recreational assistant at the local YMCA with Phil. It wasn't unusual for us to stay after hours playing indoor cricket one on one for hours on end. (We also skipped a few classes to watch reruns of *Magnum P.I.*) Phil had my back through college and ensured I didn't quit or sign off early. We had the option to start teaching with only a three-year diploma at the time, but Phil made sure I stayed on for the final year and earned my degree. I am forever grateful to him.

Be the Yin to the World's Yang

Phil Hewitt, PhD

strength and conditioning coach, University of Liverpool

I first met Hamish during my second year, and his first year, at Auckland Teachers College in the mid '90s. There were two academic pathways which could be taken: a three-year predominantly classroom-based diploma of primary teaching, and a four-year path that gave an additional qualification of a bachelor of education from Auckland University. This additional university education was almost exclusively lecture based with the method of assessment being exams and assignment based. I failed the most difficult of the second-year papers (assessment in education), which is how Hamish and I ended up in the same class. (As a side note, I lay the blame for my failure squarely at the feet of Tom Selleck and his outstanding portrayal of Thomas Magnum and on TVNZ's decision to show reruns of *Magnum P.I.* at 2:30 p.m. weekdays.)

At the end of our first year of college, we had to decide which qualification pathway we would take. One of the most important aspects of the university degree was that it recognized, and allowed for, overseas teaching. What surprised me was that as Hamish approached the decision date, and despite his confident façade, he was not going to do the university degree because of the confidence, or lack of it, that he placed in his own ability. I remember telling him that he *was* doing the bachelor's degree.

Looking back, I realize it took a lot of time to convince him that he could do the work and pass. I now understand that this attitude and opinion of his own ability were due to teachers and school counselors telling him that he wasn't smart or clever enough—a lesson for me of the influence that others' attitudes can have on a person's expectations. Some may view the negative environment that Hamish grew up in as bad, but I believe it is what drives him to do the best for his staff and students. He knows what can be achieved because he's beaten the odds. I do wonder, however, what would have happened if my *yin* had not been there to counter society's *yang*.

Right before I was about to purchase my plane tickets to England, I got the call that would change my entire educational career. A principal at Owairaka Primary, a Title I school that was incredibly diverse and had an extremely high poverty rate, where I had done my training, called and asked if I would be willing to take a job as teacher for a class that had already had two teachers quit on it. The words I remember most from that conversation are, "I don't care what happens in there. Just make sure these kids have fun and learn to love school again." *Have fun?* I thought. *Now that's what I'm talking about.* I knew that if anyone could make that happen, I was the right man for the job. Except the job wasn't just any job. The opportunity was a kindergarten placement. *Kindergarten?! Hold on a minute! I was going to be the cool fifth-grade teacher, not a kindergarten teacher.* I accepted the position only on the condition they made me a fifth-grade teacher the very next year. The principal stayed true to his word, and I moved into a fifth-grade position the following year but not before I learned some of the most important lessons of my career: 1) School should be fun and built on love; and 2) The most important ingredient is people—both big and small people.

There is a famous saying in New Zealand: "What is the most important thing in the world? It is *he tangata, he tangata, he tangata!*" (It is the people, the people, the people!) Over and over again in my life, that saying rings true. It was certainly true in my kindergarten class.

There is a famous saying in New Zealand: "What is the most important thing in the world? It is *he tangata, he tangata, he tangata!*" (It is the people, the people, the people!)

At first I had no idea what I was doing in that classroom, or how to do it! After all the planning and preparation, all I could think was, *They didn't teach me this in the textbook!* The classroom felt like being part of a professional sporting event. The game was moving so fast, and I was just trying to keep up. At the time, Teletubbies were popular with the kids, so my behavior management plan consisted of playing the Teletubbies music to get everyone to behave and listen. I felt like I was in the movie *Kindergarten Cop*! All joking aside, this experience was one of the most amazing things I had ever done for my teaching career. It truly taught me how to teach the reading and writing process, and I learned that there is no better feeling in education than watching a five-year-old's mind *click* when he or she truly gets it! It's magical! As a kindergarten teacher, I learned the power of knowing your curriculum, small-group, differentiated instruction, and how to communicate with parents—something that is a daily need with little ones!

You cannot fake your way through teaching in a kindergarten classroom; you will get run over in a heartbeat! To this day, I can remember every single student in that classroom. I worked tirelessly to help them learn and love school again. We read. We played. We even learned a Backstreet Boys song and performed it for the school. We looked pretty fly with our hair slicked back and sunglasses on! I never imagined that I would have started out as a kindergarten teacher, but I am here to tell you that *every teacher* should have a kindergarten experience.

It was during this year that I had one of the most amazing learning experiences ever. A little girl in my class with Down Syndrome changed my world and my trajectory as an educator forever. When I first came to the class, she would hide under the tables, not wanting to come out. Over time, she and I built the most amazing relationship. She taught me how to truly laugh, cry, and love! Her love was unconditional, no strings attached. When I was having a tough day, she made it better. When I needed inspiration, she inspired! This little girl taught me that when you teach through love, anything is possible, and that no matter what your circumstance is, every child needs an advocate.

I learned so much during the next four years from children, families, and colleagues whose first language was *love*. They are my *heroes*. My colleagues became friends, but as the years went on, they were actually my soulmates, my family.

No Excuses

Vaimoana Va'ai
teacher

The New Zealand decile-based funding system for schools allocates money based on the socioeconomic status of a school's geographical catchment area. Tucked away in Central Auckland, Owairaka Primary is a multicultural hub. On the New Zealand Ministry of Education website, it is rated as a decile 2 school. And when I walked through the doors the first time, I felt at home. The children's eyes greeted me with love, warmth, and a longing to learn. They were not afraid to speak their minds, tell you their home truths, and share what little they had. Their families became our family. Parents would walk their children to school, meet up with their own friends and family, and sit around in the playground and catch up like they were at home speaking in their first language. Sometimes they would come into our classrooms and sit in on our lessons. Little did they know that they were also teaching me. Approximately 60 percent of our parents had English as a second language, but the one language we all spoke that was the same was the language of love for their children. Now being a decile 2, there are times where the physical resources are hard to come by. What I found at Owairaka was that the teachers and people were the best and richest resource we had. We had a real mixture of children within our classrooms. Some of the children came from warfare countries, so we couldn't imagine what they had seen and experienced. Some of the children came from families where only one parent worked and there were multiple families staying in the house, but they came to school every day. Some of the children came from families where only they spoke English, so families relied on them to translate.

I met this crazy *palagi* (white) teacher, Hamish Brewer, fresh out of teachers college. He was energetic, motivational, and always gave 100 percent in everything he did. I knew instantly we would hit it off; I honestly thought I had found my twin. We got into trouble together because we would always push the boundaries in teaching. We wanted to offer these children enriching experiences. We were allowed to think big, and with a zero budget, we went for it.

We had a fashion show, where children created their own garments, they were models on a catwalk, and the hall was at capacity with parents cheering and some trying to jump on the catwalk to walk down with their child. We had a medieval times study, during which we transformed our classrooms into a castle and had a tournament with jousting and horse races. We needed equipment, so Hamish and some of the children collected a few shopping trolleys (carts) to be makeshift horses. One thing I know is that when Hamish wants to do something, he will not make excuses as to why it can't happen; he makes it happen.

In New Zealand, teaching always felt like fun! I loved the creativity of the curriculum, the focus on literacy, the outdoors, and the amazing culture of the New Zealand indigenous people—the Maori culture and our Pacifica people. The staff I worked with always made school feel like family; we had each other's backs, and we would have the most amazing times and experiences together ensuring we were great for kids! We would have breaks for morning tea and lunch, and during this time, staff would have duties. The two duties I loved the most were crossing guard and walking around the school ensuring everyone was playing nicely and having fun. I learned so much about relationships on crossing-guard duty. I got to know the students and their families. It was a bit like the kind of interaction I have with kids now as I greet students on their way into school each morning. Walking through the school, making sure the kids went outside to play gave me the opportunity to do my own instructional rounds. As I peered into classrooms, I could see what the various teachers had been up to. I would find great ideas and activities and work to make them my own and incorporate them into my lessons. If I had questions, I would ask the classroom teacher directly. Instructional rounds are such a powerful tool for discovery and sharing of best practices. To this day, I believe wholeheartedly in the instructional-round process. I also believe that we need to use this practice of learning from one another—and make sure that it doesn't turn into an evaluative process.

People come in and out of our lives and educational careers all the time and for a variety of reasons, and I feel fortunate to have learned from and worked for some of the very best. Two of these were administrators, Mrs. Diane (Di) Raynes and Mr. Paul Heff.

Mrs. Raynes was the first administrator to evaluate me and, boy, did she have her hands full. She taught me to take care of the details, to be accountable, and of the importance of being prepared and organized. I was great at having fun, but I learned from Mrs. Raynes that if I wanted to be taken seriously, I had to be great at planning and preparing as well. I was always amazed at her communication skills and her ability to build relationships and connections with people. Mrs. Raynes taught me a lot about life and helped me mature as an emerging teacher and adult. At twenty-five, I was always up to something, having fun, and going out. She made me aware of my need to find balance. I admired the way she treated everyone with respect and dignity. She did her work with a smile and would be direct and honest in her feedback.

I remember as a young teacher that I would raise my voice a little too much. To this day, I can hear her telling me, "Your voice is not a behavior management system." If I wanted to make it in teaching, she said I needed to adjust my tone in the classroom. Otherwise I wouldn't have a voice or career much longer!

Another thing I admired about Mrs. Raynes was her power to uplift the kids. They knew her as the "Purple Maniac." Her favorite color was purple, and she had a golden box where the names of students who were doing amazing things were collected. Throughout the year, those were drawn out, and the students received a reward. The Purple Maniac could command the crowd! I saw the power she had to create a culture of celebration and identity. The students loved her and would go crazy when she entered the room. I wanted to be like that!

A Rebel with a Cause

Di Raynes
principal, colleague, friend

Every once in a while, a teacher who is just a bit different—in a good way—comes along to work in your school. They understand kids and can connect with them at their level. They bring about change because kids know they are loved and valued and listened to. These teachers teach and lead with heart, with integrity, and with a belief that every child can succeed! Hamish Brewer is one of these educators extraordinaire!

I had the privilege of working with Hamish when he first became a teacher. From the very beginning, Hamish was different. He always ignored the white noise in education and put the kids first. He gave them a sense of belonging; every kid knew they were safe with Mr. Brewer as their teacher. He had their backs. He listened. He valued. He gave kids a sense of self-worth and made learning fun! Kids excelled in his class because they trusted him. They knew that he understood them and believed in them. These were kids from disadvantaged backgrounds who had lived a lifetime before they were ten years old. Hamish gave them the gifts of hope and self-belief. I loved working alongside this guy because he put people first: kids, parents, and colleagues. He made everyone feel valued and gave credit where credit was due. He had crazy, out-there ideas that inspired kids and made them (and the adults too!) want to come to school every day.

Teachers make a difference for kids. When you make a difference for kids, you make a difference for adults, which makes a difference in and for communities. Teachers are social engineers. We create the future, and when you lead from the heart and with love, that has to create positive, nurturing communities. This is the work Hamish does. Hamish isn't here to be average; he is here to be amazing, but he won't do this on his own because Hamish believes in taking his colleagues with him on his journey. Lift as you climb! Gandhi said, "Be the change you wish to see in the world." Hamish is the change. He is creating communities filled with hope, grown from love. I'm proud to call Hamish my friend, and I love the fact that he is now teaching me a thing or two!

Mr. Heff was an off-the-chain, eccentric, wild, creative, and visionary leader who lived outside the box. We were made for each other. Before his retirement, Mr. Heff gave me the green light. He encouraged me to be a maverick who embraced people and taught on fire. We would spend hours sharing and talking about leadership, branding, teamwork, and having fun in schools. He was so far ahead of his time when it came to incorporating those ideas into a school. We called our school "The Greatest Little School in the Universe." Together, we would always be looking at how we could do something bigger and bolder than had ever been done before.

Mr. Heff referred to me as *Grasshopper* and gave me my first opportunity in leadership. He did not believe in redshirting leaders. His thought was it didn't matter what your age or experience was; what mattered was whether you could do the job. And he knew I could. The lessons I learned from Mr. Heff continue to serve me well as an administrator today.

Dave Burgess wrote *Teach Like a Pirate*, but if we know anything about the open seas and a pirate life, it's that there are many pirates out there. Just like Dave, we want to grow them all because if we can get people teaching on fire and teaching with authentic, relevant learning experiences, then we all win. Most importantly, kids win. I like to think that I am one of the original pirates, but the truth is there have been many pirates over the years, some heard, some seen, and some feared and loved. What is exciting about the day and age that we live in now is that technology gives us a way to connect with and learn from those pirates wherever they are.

DO SOMETHING DIFFERENT

Ever since I first set foot in the classroom, I was coming up with unique and authentic experiences for students that were relevant and engaging to them. Here are a couple of favorites that you could implement:

Student-Led Fashion Show

Never pass up the opportunity to integrate your lesson and learning across content areas. It's one powerful way to create rich and engaging experiences. In my second or third year of teaching, we were looking at technology, design, angles, brochures, and posters. The lesson we were doing felt drab, so the teachers I worked with and I thought, *How can we go big*? The answer was an event, and what better event than a futuristic fashion show, set at night, and while we are at it, let's turn it into a musical with all the latest beats! We were going to make it gritty, loud, edgy, and exciting! We gathered up all the students, shared the plan, and went to work preparing, designing, and producing a fashion show to end all fashion shows. Every student got to choose their role: We needed lighting, costume changes, costume designers, food, directors, producers, a marketing team, and the list went on and on.

The students collaborated in groups, and every student felt a sense of pride, passion, and purpose in the work we were doing. The learning went on for weeks, and the students did not miss a beat. The costume and set designs were amazing. The students decorated the gym space, designed a stage, got the equipment for lighting, found a DJ, and set up the space. They rehearsed again and again until they felt they were ready for the show. What I enjoyed most was collaborating on this project with my grade-level teachers. We ended up being facilitators as students owned and led their learning. It was perfect. The students went on to finish the show with a special song and individual candles to create a special moment with their parents or caregivers.

The America's Cup

The America's Cup is one of the oldest yachting regattas in the world; it is considered the Formula One of yachting. Technological advances have only increased the performance, high-level grandstanding, and politics that are part of the legend that is the America's Cup. In New Zealand, we participate in this event with a sense of national point of pride—it's us against the world! New Zealand against the big money of the other syndicates around the world, like Prada from Italy. Like the Olympics, the event takes place every four years. It is hosted by the holder of the cup at the time, which just happened to be New Zealand when we came up with a plan to hold our own America's Cup. Our school was near the ocean, so *why not?!* It was a way to take a major event and integrate it into our classroom learning in an authentic and relevant way.

Every class designed and built its own boat for the race. It really was a STEAM project if I ever saw one. It included all the chaos, competition, innovation, and psychological warfare that the real America's Cup offered. In the weeks leading up to our regatta, students investigated and researched everything related to boat building. The only stipulations were that the boats could not be powered by any motor system, and they could not be an actual boat—a canoe, for example.

The America's Cup was famous for being secretive, and our school fell right into this rabbit hole. As designs started to come together, it was awesome watching all the innovation and ideas come to life, including floating bathtubs, rafts, and all sorts of flotation devices. My class developed a floating platform, and we deviated to the dark side a little and tried to stuff Styrofoam into the hull of the boat to support its ability to float. Just like the participants of the real-word America's Cup, we were trying to manipulate the rules. Another class found out and protested the use of this material on our boat because it was seen as a flotation aid. The rules committee elected to side with the class who laid the protest, and we were required to remove the foam.

Race day was amazing! We took the entire school down to the beach to watch the boats race. (Yes, we had the fire department out for safety, and we all wore safety gear.) The races began with lots of excitement and noise. My class had the fastest boat, but we struggled to stay afloat once we started taking on water and fell behind. If memory serves me right, we came in third. The learning and experience for the students were amazing, from development to sailing. It crossed all curriculum areas and kept our students highly engaged as it promoted creativity, problem-solving, and critical thinking.

Turn Your Classroom into a City

For about four months, we turned our entire classroom into a city—an experience that hit on every curriculum area. We started out with some math by looking at perimeter, area, and space. We also considered societies in social studies, which quickly led to us designing concept cities on paper and then using masking tape to scale them on the floor for the city. As a class, we discussed pollution and challenges of cities around the world. Students researched the effects of urbanization and how recycling can be a positive contributor to society. The unit just kept evolving organically from concept to concept as students learned until one day during art class, one of the students said, "Mr. Brewer, why don't we turn our classroom into a city?"

Of course, I said, "Why not? How are we going to do it?"

After a couple hours of brainstorming, we all agreed, "Let's do it!"

In the days that followed, the students had their parents excited and engaged about the project as well. We put out a request for materials and quickly received refrigerator boxes, crates, pallets, wood, and all sorts of materials. The only stipulation I set with the students was that if the city project negatively impacted our ability to learn and stay focused, we had to stop. Do you think that happened? Nope! A month later, we had a fully functioning city in our room, complete with a post office to deliver mail and a phone system (using strings and cups). All the students had jobs and responsibilities. There was even a newspaper where students collected articles for print.

My favorite learning that took place came when students decided they couldn't see very well. The city was dark and the buildings darker. I saw this need and collected every piece of the school's electricity science equipment that I could find and dumped it in the middle of the park. Yes, we had a park in the city. The students learned how to put circuits together so they could run battery-powered lights between the buildings in the city. From that point forward, we had students working jobs as electricians.

Another special moment was when our city's librarian began surveying the citizens about the books they wanted to read. By having a voice in the books that were in the library, the entire class got engaged in reading!

Memories That Matter

Neki Mewes
student at the time of the Classroom City project

Mr. Brewer was my teacher seventeen years ago at Laingholm Primary in New Zealand. He made a huge impact on my life. I can remember him being a super fun, carefree (but strict when needed) teacher and friend.

I remember one day he turned up in class with mountains of cardboard taller than we were as ten-year-olds. He told us we were going to build a fully functioning city right there in our classroom. You can imagine the excitement on our faces. We were told to pair up and think of a business we wanted to run. My friends and I decided we would be the city's post office (posties). Along with our post office, there was a newspaper, an electrician, and a pet shop. I remember the newspaper was delivered to us (the post shop) in the mornings. We would then set off delivering the newspaper to the different stores along with letters and packages people wanted sent to different places around the classroom. I remember the electrician was making lights with basic little battery-to-bulb terminals, and the pet shop had fish and axolotls you could go visit and feed. It was a great way for us children to get insight into how the world worked; it made the learning real.

Mr. Brewer was a teacher I always remembered. He made learning fun and different, and sometimes all kids need is to look at things from a different perspective. I was very lucky to have him as a teacher and would be privileged if he was my child's teacher. He is making a huge change in education.

The students investigated what made cities run, from town-hall meetings, to protests, down to designing a recycling and garbage program to ensure our city was clean. On a funny note, the students decided that my space was a dilapidation and had to be torn down, so they removed my desk and redesigned the area to better meet the needs of the city students.

The key, for the teacher and educator in the room, is to recognize the teachable moments that can be nurtured into organic learning experiences—cultivating them and then letting them run their course. The beauty of education and learning is that it can be as amazing, authentic, and engaging as we want to make it or let it become. As educators and adults in the building, we can be the very thing or problem that gets in the way of amazing learning experiences taking place, and we have to ensure this is not the case.

You can see by integrating our curriculums, using real-life scenarios and connections, and thinking big and broad, we have the opportunity to create something special. What truly makes the learning experience *next level* is when we make it authentic and relevant for students. This realness fosters excitement and engagement. Students no longer respond to compliant learning. But when they are engaged and participating the process of active learning, that's when the magic happens.

I hope that a takeaway from this chapter is that we appreciate the amazing resources, teachers, educators, and leaders around us. We can draw inspiration from the person across the hallway, from each other, or from another school. Let's take education off the island and join forces. It's time to stop hiding great instruction; it's time to celebrate the excellence around us and let it run free. Let's come out from the shadows and celebrate together. All students deserve our very best, and all schools deserve to succeed. When we build a strong network of relationships, we can make it happen!

7

THE TRUTH AND FALLACIES OF SCHOOL IMPROVEMENT

U nlocking school improvement has been a holy grail for schools, researchers, politicians, and educators alike. The challenge is not new to today's generation, nor is it unique to any one area. In speaking with educators and education leaders in schools around the world, I've seen firsthand that school improvement is a need everywhere. It doesn't matter if you are in the highest socioeconomic school setting or are working with some of your country's most at-risk students, educators across the planet are trying to close the achievement gap and improve school processes and outcomes. In that crucial pursuit, some educators end up chasing the latest and greatest fads—which are often simply recycled ideas that may not have even worked the first time around.

For years, our efforts for school improvement have focused on providing resources, money, programs, and more new, shiny ideas to create better outcomes for both schools and students. What I can tell you with 100 percent certainty is that programs don't fix kids—or schools for that matter. You cannot replace the most amazing teacher with a program or strategy. We cannot take the approach of throwing ideas like spaghetti against the wall to see what sticks. Our students deserve better than that.

For years, school improvement has been caught in between what the state and federal governments demand in terms of immediate accomplishments and what it takes to improve scores and close the achievement gap long term. The reality is that implementing an improvement process takes anywhere from three to five years with a well-executed, thought-out plan that has a laser focus on the identified areas of weakness and growth. It is never an instant fix. And it is never just about test scores.

For years, I felt as if our worth as schools and educators was determined by our students' results on end-of-year exams. But that is just not true. Test scores are *one* data point for us to consider on our journey of school improvement. Turning a school around requires so much more. Improving culture, practices, instruction, brand, and engagement work together to make our schools better. Eventually, success in those areas leads to improved student achievement on tests. It is important to note, however, that school improvement does not begin or end with test scores.

For years, school improvement has become more challenging for schools, school leaders, and communities as we struggle to find answers to increasingly difficult scenarios and situations such as student populations that are coming to school having faced trauma, malnutrition, single-parent families, poverty, and mental and physical abuse. The challenges, however, are not limited to low-socioeconomic schools and communities. Our affluent communities are facing many of the same challenges including the silent conversation that is taking place where these issues are purposely hidden. Students live in fear of sharing their concerns or asking for assistance.

The conversation around and research about school improvement focused in recent years on the topics of student achievement, principal impact, parent engagement, professional learning communities, class size, and teacher impact. None of these are bad things, but when schools try to accomplish everything at once, the effect is teachers and school leaders are spread too thin. While trying to cover and master so many areas, we end up mastering none and repeating the cycle struggling for improvement. As schools tackle tremendous challenges, they are faced with declining enrollment, staff turnover, reduced funds, fewer resources, and low morale. Something has to change.

Over the years, I have helped multiple schools at multiple levels do what people call a *turnaround*. Before leading and turning around schools at the elementary and middle school levels, I observed and worked in several turnaround schools. In the process, I realized that "more" does not equal "more success." And by adding more (programs, PLCs, meetings, layers, and resources, etc.), we actually end up suffocating and stymieing the school improvement process altogether.

The assumption that a school's zip code determines its outcome drives me insane. I am on a mission to disrupt this thinking and to blow this theory completely up. I am driven to prove the world wrong about the limitations that are so easily placed on schools where poverty or students of color are the norm. I understand that working with and in at-risk schools is not for everyone, but it is for me. I know my lane, and I'm staying in it. Anything that the nay-sayers think, write, or say about my school and our students only fuels my fire to see us win. I still carry a chip on my shoulder from my upbringing and a lifetime of people telling me I wasn't good enough or wouldn't amount to much. Author and UCLA Professor Pedro Noguera often shares during his speeches that poverty is not a learning disability. He's right! My life proves it. My students prove it every day. No one has to be defined by their zip code, poverty, race, religion, or experiences.

Closing the achievement gap is about all schools. Being the difference for all students cannot be about talk; catchy phrases won't cut it. All too often, people want to talk about the work that needs to be done. We are fantastic at planning, but we struggle with action and follow-through. We have to do the work! Turning schools around takes action. It requires that we stand up for all students. Improving your school is not a one-week thing; it's not a September beginning-of-the-year thing. It's a daily commitment to changing the game and disrupting the norm. It's an everyday thing! I strive for a gang mentality with my teachers, schools, and stakeholders—including parents. We have to go all-in or not at all. While generally I would agree anything associated with gangs is not good, I do love the concept of a group of people coming together with a common mission and a sense of committed unity. When the members of your school community are willing to sacrifice it all for the mission and each other, you become unstoppable.

With our students' well-being and futures at stake, there are no second chances. Our students are counting on us. There must be a sense of urgency around the work we do, because every day, we are working to save students' lives.

CLOSING THE ACHIEVEMENT GAP

When it comes to closing the achievement gap and turning schools around, I believe there are some small areas of focus that can make the dream a reality. It's not rocket science, although there are plenty of expensive "experts" and "programs" out there that would have you think otherwise.

- **Build a simple bridge.** It's easy to make the mistake of overthinking *everything*. We have turned education into a Pinterest board. Educators rewrite the curriculum all the time because they want to "pretty" it up. Stop rewriting the curriculum. The curriculum is written; just teach it! The fact of the matter is you can't teach a curriculum if you don't know it. School improvement is about knowing exactly what you have to teach, how you are going to teach it, and how you are going assess it to find out what your students know and don't know. It's as simple as that! When you teach the curriculum with relevant, authentic, and real experiences, you will completely change the trajectory of your school and the stakeholders in it. The problem with Pinteresting education and reinventing the curriculum is that teachers lose sight of the target and then wonder why their students struggle. The students struggle because we stop teaching the appropriate curriculum differentiated to meet the needs of our students. When you know the curriculum, understand your students' needs, and know their starting point, you can begin to build a bridge that closes the achievement gap.

- **Keep the main thing the main thing.** The number-one goal I have when I go into or work with a school is to keep the main idea the main idea by keeping things simple. Educational leaders make a common mistake when they go into a new school or assignment: They want to make their mark, put

When you know the curriculum, understand your students' needs, and know their starting point, you can begin to build a bridge that closes the achievement gap.

their stamp on the way they think things should or shouldn't be done. The problem with this is that often these new or young administrators have very little experience. Reading a book (or several) may help, but remember that what works for some won't work for all. You really have to take knowledge, ideas, programs, and processes and make them work for you. You cannot plug someone else's solution into your school's issue and expect to be successful. Your job when going into a new school, regardless of your title, is to be an archaeologist. You are digging for information and seeking to understand the current climate, practice, and processes. Unless you find something negligent or that impacts kids in a negative way, do not change anything—yet.

- **Remember, relationships are key.** You cannot implement effective change in an educational setting without first establishing a relationship with those around you; the staff, students, and community have to trust and respect you. Respect is earned; it's not given, and it goes two ways. If you think your positional authority is going give you automatic credibility or respect, then you just signed your ticket out! Do not be quick to pass judgment on the people, stakeholders, or practices that are currently in place. Once you find understanding and have established a connection where stakeholders do not fear voicing their opinions and giving you feedback, then you can truly have the impact you desire.

- **Celebrate what's good.** Something that gets left out of school is celebrating what is successful. It's easy to find and point out what is wrong, but you also need to look for and celebrate what is great. Success and change can occur when people have a positive mindset and outlook. I choose to blow right by the negativity and, instead, focus on and celebrate the areas and people who model excellence. Point out those who are positive about being the difference for all kids.

FOUR FUNDAMENTAL ISSUES TO FACE

In almost every school in need of a turnaround, there are four fundamental issues. I'm not talking about the obvious indicators that a school is in trouble, like high staff turnover, student absenteeism, or discipline issues, all of which are important and have an impact on your school. I'm talking about the issues that go unaddressed because people are too scared to have an open and honest dialogue about them:

1. Lack of belief in students
2. Blame for failure placed on students
3. Blame on everyone else but themselves
4. A mentality of "this is how we have always done it"

What stands out in these four issues is that the problem is not the students! Unfortunately, sometimes it's the adults in these schools who get in the way of students and schools succeeding. Many times it's not a question of effort or want on the adults' part, it's just that their efforts are misguided and in need of direction and vision.

We have to be open to change and be ready to grow and evolve. It's not okay to keep doing the same thing because that's the way we have always done it or because you're not prepared to go a little bit further. Put in the work that's necessary to be successful. School improvement is not achieved through a gimmick or by instituting a new program. It's not about more; it's about grit, determination, focus, having a clear plan that is laid out with the steps to success for both the long term and short term.

What I cannot and will not accept in my school or from those around me is negativity, drama, or excuses. It's easy to blame everyone else for our shortcomings or to find fault or excuses for why things are not going the way we need them to go. I am not looking for excuses; I'm looking for solutions because our kids are counting on us each and every day. We are in the business of saving and changing lives, which means we don't have a moment to lose. So many of our students can look around and find an excuse right in front of them. Our schools must not be another opportunity for a student to see an excuse or a reason to give up.

GET THE RIGHT PEOPLE ON BOARD

One of the first things I tell my staff or someone I am hiring is, "I have no interest in drama, negativity, or gossip. We don't want drama, and we won't accept drama." Along these lines, when I interview someone for a position in my building, I let them know up front what the expectations are concerning everything from behaviors and planning to instruction. I purposely set the expectation from the very beginning so that everyone knows how serious I am about the effort and dedication required for this work. I don't use a script in the interview. I'd rather evaluate people by looking in their eyes and hearing from their hearts. Neither do I ask questions about reading and writing. I am more interested in who the person is in front of me. I want to know if they are willing to fight for my kids and me. My team and I can teach others the expectations for instruction, so I focus on questions that concern tenacity, determination, and heart. The questions are like *What is the greatest challenge you have ever overcome?* My goal, when talking to an applicant, is to ensure they completely understand what the expectation is going to be around teamwork, instruction, commitment, and our mission. Sometimes this has led to teachers turning down jobs with us over the years, but it's also ensured that we have hired the right people to do the enormous work we do.

One of those "right people" is Mr. Annunziata. I knew within a minute that I wanted to hire him. He talked about loyalty, and I was sold. I am blessed he said yes!

As a leader in any organization, you do not have time to get the hiring process wrong because people are counting on you, and it's hard to undo a bad hire.

All-In!

Mr. Annunziata
teacher/athletic director

Unsatisfied with the status quo, I had been going through the motions and was considering leaving the profession. In 2016, Mr. Brewer was named principal at Fred Lynn. A colleague who knew him told me that she thought he and I would work well together. I reached out about a posted position, and within a half hour, I was driving over for an interview. When asked about my philosophy, I bluntly laid it all on the table. I wanted to teach, to change the world, to build kids up. I wanted to make Fred Lynn the place to be. In short, if he wanted a robot, I wasn't his guy. The interview took less than a minute before he opened his laptop and asked how to spell my name. Hamish allows me to be me, tattoos, motorcycle club, and all. I feel empowered and *all-in* for our students. Thanks to Hamish Brewer, I am changing the world, building relationships, and impacting the lives of students who need teachers who do it a little differently.

UNCOVER THE REAL PROBLEM(S)

How do you find out what the challenges and strengths are in a school? When you go into new a school, what's your plan? You cannot presume to know and understand how things have gone. Sometimes what looks like the problem or the challenge from the outside ends up being very different once you get on the inside. Earlier in this chapter, I said not to change anything when you start at a new school—particularly if you are in a leadership position. Your job is to be an archaeologist. You are on a fact-finding mission. Your research can start by providing stakeholders with a voice. One way to do that is by giving them a place to provide feedback. I put out a drop box and a short survey with space for comments. The two questions that I ask are . . .

1. What are the three things you love most about your school?
2. What are the three things you would love to grow at your school?

Without fail, the feedback to these two questions will set you up for immediate success. The answers provide you with actionable items for improvement. You do not want feedback that is not actionable, nor do you need rants. The way these two questions are worded ensures that I get feedback that I can work with. By asking the stakeholders, "What are the three things you would love to grow at your school?" I get answers from a positive mindset, rather than with words like *hate, change,* or *dislike,* which automatically drum up negative feelings. Using a word like *grow* sets a tone of opportunity and renewal.

During my beginning years of teaching, my principal, Mr. Heff, introduced me to the "Fish Philosophy" that stems from the Pike Fish Market in Seattle, Washington. The fishmongers in the shop throw fish around. The amazing love for the work they do and for their customers is inspiring. I was fortunate enough to visit the fish market and had a blast watching the team in full effect. They have four guiding principles:

1. Play.
2. Make someone's day.
3. Choose your attitude.
4. Be there.

At every school I have led since that visit, the first book I share with the staff is *Fish!*. It's not about being a better teacher or school leader, although if you apply its principles, you will 100 percent improve your craft and practices. The reason for this is that school improvement has a winning start with relationships and good people. It couldn't be more important to have the right people in place with the right attitude. That's what *Fish!* and the team at the Pike Fish Market are all about.

You have to ignore the noise and all the things that you cannot control. You cannot control, for example, what happens when students leave school, who their parents are, or what their circumstances are. You can only control what is right in front of you, what is in the moment. You can only control what happens from the first school bell in the morning to the last school bell of the day. When your team can finally let go of the things that they cannot control, they are liberated to focus their energy on what they *can* control. Attitude is a good place to start.

My favorite tip when it comes to ego, personal agendas, and attitude may sound like a recording on repeat. That's okay. I'll keep repeating it: You get to choose your attitude every day. You are the sole person responsible for your attitude, and how you choose your attitude impacts everyone with whom you come into contact. By choosing your attitude every day and leaving your ego at the door, you are saying that you are putting those around you first and that your sole focus is on the amazing children right in front of you. With that kind of attitude and focus, you give yourself the opportunity to be amazing each and every day—the chance to be the difference for students. When we are able to do this collectively, our schools can become unstoppable.

When educators are having fun and being present, they become mindful of one another and of each person's needs. When you are present, you notice ways to uplift the people around you. You figure out how best to work together on behalf of the children. Being present is in the details; it's the little things, like coming prepared to a planning meeting, doing small, random acts of kindness, or standing in a hallway when it's easier to sit at your desk. Being present is about being engaged with your students—conferencing when you don't have to, reading with students while they are reading. This kind of mindfulness shows up in your attention to the details of the work you do each and every day. Try dropping a small note off for a colleague, or leave a sticky note on someone's door who did something special. These small gestures of being present uplift the entire team and building.

Choose Your Attitude

Eric Ewald
principal

It was the spring of 2016. Mentally, I wasn't in a great place. I was in the midst of my first year leading a new school, and it was not all sunshine and rainbows. Student behavior was taking a toll on our staff. They were taking their toll on me, too, which didn't help the situation.

Enter Hamish Brewer. I don't remember the specifics for how we connected, but I do know that it was through the original #PrincipalsInAction Voxer group. We hit it off instantly; group Voxes led to side Voxes, text messages, phone calls, and eventually a face-to-face meeting.

Through our conversations, Hamish introduced me to a couple of things that changed the game for me. First and foremost, he shared the book *Fish!*. Hamish told me it was a resource that he required all staff members to read when attempting to change the culture of his school. I was intrigued. Fast-forward several years, and I can still distinctly remember reading this book. I finished it in a single sitting and completely covered the book with highlights, marks, and notes to myself. It is one of the top personal development books that I've ever read.

Fish! shares four principles: Be there, Choose your attitude, Make someone's day, and Play. The principle that stood out the most to me, due to conversations with Hamish and my own circumstances, was Choose your attitude. I remember Hamish telling me, "When you come through the doors each and every day, choose your attitude. You own it. Nobody else does; that's up to you."

Since developing a relationship with Hamish and utilizing the resources and wisdom that he shared with me, I've been a more optimistic and positive person. I know that while I don't always choose my circumstances, I always choose my attitude. And I believe that adopting this mindset is some of the best school reform available.

Before he became known as the tattooed, skateboarding principal, he was a mentor and a friend to me. He is an educator and a person whom I greatly admire for his relentlessness, his attitude, his kind heart, and his authentic personality. I am fortunate that he came into my life when he did to share with me his take on the Choose Your Attitude mantra.

MAKE THE MOST OF MEETINGS

I am not a huge fan of meetings. In general, I think organizations meet way too often, rehash the same conversations, and close with no actionable items and no accountability for who is going to do what. We have to stop the madness!

Staff meetings can be valuable, but too much of the time, they focus on the do's and don'ts and end up being a negative experience. What a waste! In a ten-month school year, you may get an opportunity to speak to your entire staff ten to fifteen times as a whole group. So make those meetings count! You can make that time valuable in terms of motivation and inspiration by repeating your vision and mission. Celebrate what's going well, and highlight the teachers and staff members who are positively impacting your school. In short, lift people up . . . and keep the meeting short! Everyone has work to do, so don't keep your people tied up in a meeting any longer than is necessary or effective. I focus my energy on some of the following types of meetings: Feedback, Planning, and Drops.

Make Feedback Meaningful

I tried for years to figure out how to look at grades in a meaningful way beyond providing performance feedback to students and parents. Then one day, an idea hit me: *What if there is a correlation between report-card grades and state testing?* Could classroom grades predict success on state exams? Excited by this idea, I began to investigate by teacher, by grade, and by year. I quickly found that there were definite trends: trends by subject, trends by time of the year, and in many cases, trends by teachers.

Looking at these trends helped me see how variable our instruction and planning was. It also showed me that we didn't have common understanding and expectations around grading. This prompted our administrative teams and PLCs to dig deeper about consistency of instruction and assessment. The results were powerful, horizontal- and vertical-team teacher conversations that transformed our collective grading and instruction process. These conversations ensured that our teachers were aware of the practices across all grade levels. That knowledge as well as understanding the instructional philosophies and strategies that were necessary to be successful as a school empowered them to offer our students the best possible instruction. But first, we had to get to the place where our educators felt safe and not threatened by the conversation. Once we crossed that bridge, people were open for dialogue, and the conversations were eye opening!

The data and information became so powerful that when students took tests, we could see and target those who were on the cusp of success and just needed a little push to get over the hump. We could gauge and identify what our lowest range and highest range for performance on a state test would be, and we could cross-reference that, for example, against our developmental reading assessments. The alignment was unbelievable! What I loved most, aside from the predictors that could tell us if we were on track, was that we could see ways to better align our practices, instruction, and expectations to be consistent across the board. Throughout the year, we would post our results and grades in a spreadsheet, and then review each teacher's grades along with each grade level's scores in our data-review meetings. With no shame and no blame, these meetings felt safe, focused, and inspiring.

From there, we worked on making grades meaningful to the students. Feedback should be intentional, focused, and actionable. If feedback is final, students feel like they are defined by a grade, especially if we don't give them guidelines for improvement. *How can a student improve if they don't know what they need to improve on or if all they ever receive in feedback is a letter or number?* When we only used grades as feedback for our students' performance, the only indicators we had were numbers or letters that told us and the students one thing: what they got. When we worked as a school to deconstruct what that feedback meant, we were able to use the data to help students succeed. We began requiring conferencing with students and parents not just in areas of reading but across all curriculum areas. As teachers engaged their students in constructive conversations about their grades, the focused and meaningful feedback helped us close the achievement gap. When students (and teachers) know the target, they go for it!

Planning with Professional Learning Communities

Professional learning communities (PLCs) are smaller, focused groups of educators who meet throughout the year to discuss content-specific teaching, and they can have a huge impact on a school. Effective PLCs eliminate silos by engaging everyone in the group. Each teacher in a PLC takes ownership of the process of designing authentic, relevant instructional experiences for students. As they discuss and plan, they should draw on data-based decision-making to guide the process—all with a focus on improving school performance and outcomes. With those parameters in place, I've seen amazing results come out of PLCs. When schools implement a PLC's strategies, structures, and processes, the result can be laser-focused action.

How to Ensure That PLCs Are Effective

1. **Do not make meeting a cumbersome process.** I've seen some schools make the mistake of turning PLC meetings into a weeklong marathon laden in heavy paperwork.

2. **Put teachers in charge of PLC meetings.** If you want to invite a specialist to the meeting, that's fine. But I always insist that the teachers own and run the meeting and that the specialists contribute input as needed. When teachers take ownership of the meeting, they value the process. Aside from that, our teachers must be the content experts. If a specialist is always there spoon-feeding the teachers information, they won't own it. Plus, the teachers are the ones in the trenches. They will have the best understanding of what their students need and what it will take to execute the plan.

3. **Maintain focus on what's important.** There is such a difference between the urgent and the important. If you are a leader, encourage your school's PLCs to stay laser focused on the target. If you are part of a PLC, be intentional about keeping the main thing the main thing. Our groups typically start with these questions:
   - What do the children have to know?
   - How are we going to teach it?
   - If they don't get it, how are we going to make sure they do?

4. **Push for deeper understanding of the content.** After unpacking the standard in question, the teachers look for

the essential learning: key concepts, vocabulary, etc. From there, they work backward to create the plan.

When you initially implement this process of PLC planning, pushing for deeper content understanding from your teachers is a good practice. One way I've done this is to ask the teachers to look at the objective from the curriculum and tell me how much they know about it. The teachers would then share their responses, including the ways they have taught the objective in the past. With those ideas on the table, we would then open the curriculum document and unpack the objective. That's when the *aha* moments happened around the table. I could see the light bulbs come on as the teachers realized they really only had a biased, superficial understanding of the objective and that there was so much content that they had been missing. This exercise would always set us up for success.

5. **Allow for individuality.** After the planning process, I never require that the agreed-upon plan has to look the same from classroom to classroom. Demanding uniformity restricts individuality, expression, and may well prevent teachers from meeting the needs of the individuals in their unique room. What I do insist on is that every teacher is on the same page. With a clear plan in place, teachers can teach the same material *and* use their individual talents and creativity to do so.

What you find with a well-organized and planned PLC, while you let teachers know that they can and should have individual flair, the teachers tend to be on the same page for instruction and look more alike than what they set out to do.

Trusted to Teach

Mrs. Dziuba
seventh-grade teacher

It was my third year as a fourth-grade teacher. I was team lead, working twelve hours a day at school, and spending all my planning periods in long meetings writing word-for-word lesson plans for new teachers on my team. As much as I love helping others, I was definitely spreading myself thin. Even more, despite our hours of planning and preparation, we were still struggling in most of the core content areas. I began questioning my career choice, wondering how I could put so much of myself into something that felt so, at times, ineffectual.

On top of all my doubts, I'd go home to my roommate telling me tales of tribal ceremonies, amazing test scores, and of supportive teams and principals. Her school's structure outlined time to plan and prepare at work, so she brought less home. When, one day, she approached me about a fourth-grade position at her school, I jumped at the opportunity. I went, I interviewed, and I got offered the job. Though the thought of leaving my students and fellow teachers was difficult, I knew I wanted to be a part of a school that was doing something truly exciting and unheard of in the education world.

So I decided I would take the chance and go and teach fourth grade. During our initial work week, I realized how tightly knit the staff really was and how motivational Mr. Brewer truly is. After only those five days, I cried at how excited I was to actually get to teach again—in the right environment. That year, my entire outlook on teaching changed. I had a team that helped with resources and planning, a principal who trusted me as an educator, and the freedom to do activities above and beyond the ordinary. I *loved* teaching again. The simple fact that everyone was all-in really made the difference in my experience. Mr. Brewer helped me see what I was truly capable of, and for that, I will always be grateful.

Let Educators Own the Process

You cannot create a school culture that is driven by innovation, creativity, collaboration, and initiative if *every single time* a decision needs to be made, it has to go through the boss's or principal's office. That is just one of the many reasons that I am a firm believer in flat leadership. A school principal, or leader of any kind, cannot possibly be in every place at once. Since you cannot clone yourself, you have to build trust and capacity in your building for educators or employees to feel confident about making decisions and executing plans. When they understand your mission and vision, the decisions become easy. I've found that if you trust your educators to own the planning and execution process as well as the outcome, they will almost always make the best decision in support of the direction you are going as a school.

Filling Someone's Bucket (Drops)

Drops are such an important example of something small that can have huge impact. They are a way to model for staff what it looks like to celebrate your school's successes no matter how big or small. As an assistant principal, I got to work under Jewell Moore. She introduced me to drops, and I have celebrated Fridays with my staff every week since. We gather all the staff on Fridays to reflect on our successes for the week and share in everyone's wins. Each Friday, a faculty member gives out a drop to someone as a sign of gratitude for something that person did. It starts at the beginning of the year with the administration giving out the first drops. If you receive a drop, it is your responsibility to give one to someone else the following week.

All too often, schools go weeks without coming together as a collective to celebrate, laugh, cry, and love. When we gather weekly for this short but impactful time each Friday afternoon, it uplifts everyone so that we can finish the week on a high. Drops are a wonderful way to take a break from the hustle and bustle of the week. They provide a few minutes to pause and recognize one another and to chat with people from other areas of the campus. During these weekly meetings, we share and celebrate the fun stuff, like baby announcements and engagements. And when someone is in need, we use this time to round up the troops and put a plan in place for a meal delivery, for example. The one rule for these Friday meetings is that there are no reminders or notes around rules, expectations, or coming events. This time is strictly for celebration and community.

Schools that are failing or struggling often suffer from a lack of culture and community. When you create opportunities for community, you begin to build and foster a culture of family and connection that extends well beyond the school day. Culture, grounded in positive relationships, is essential to any school's success. Don't mistake *culture* for a catchphrase. It is something you must lead and work on all year long. Drops are one positive way to feed your school's culture.

STAY FOCUSED ON WHAT MATTERS MOST

I have long been passionate about the "effective schools" research that began with Ron Edmonds back in the 1970s. I believe this work is relevant and meaningful in today's educational landscape and offers a guide to educators who want to see positive, dramatic change in their schools. Through my doctoral studies at Virginia Tech, I formed a deep understanding of the principles of effective schools, worked to grow them, and noticed that these are the same strategies and principles I implemented in the schools I have worked through the years.

When working on a school turnaround—or to improve any school, for that matter—ask yourself if these seven attributes exist in your school today as a focus and expectation:

1. Acquisition of basic skills
2. Safe and orderly environment
3. High expectations
4. Strong instructional leadership
5. Pupil progress monitoring and planning
6. Authentic, relevant learning experiences
7. Fun

These seven fundamentals for success are interrelated and essential for an effective, thriving school. If any of these are missing, your school cannot operate at maximum capacity. Honestly, it is easy enough to find at least a couple of them in every school. The trick is bringing all seven into sharp focus and using them to move your school from good to great—or from failing to succeeding.

As the instructional leader in my school, I know that making sure these areas stay in focus is a responsibility that starts and ends with me—but it is not all up to me alone. The same is true for any leader. As leaders, we must set the stage for success. A quality leader doesn't wait for someone else to provide the answer. If you are waiting on help from outside your school, understand this: Help isn't coming! You and your team are the cavalry! Effective change starts and ends right in the school. The central office is not the answer. They can offer feedback, support, and services, and your administrators can provide assistance. But they are not the answer. It takes the entire team within the school—with that gang mentality—to go after every single child. I learned to be an effective leader when I realized that it didn't have to be all about me; I didn't have to do it all. I was only one person, but once I engaged my stakeholders and created an environment for teachers to have a voice and to own their school and the practices and processes we implemented, that's when we excelled.

While we can lay the foundation for school improvement with some solid core principles and instructional processes, the building process never really stops. It truly does take three to five *years* to implement and achieve a school turnaround. There are no shortcuts, and it takes the entire organization's effort. School improvement takes all stakeholders wholeheartedly believing that every single child can learn and that you can be successful as a school. It's a mindset, and it has to become a way of life. We cannot be afraid to have the tough conversations and ask the hard questions to move forward. No shame, no blame, just solutions and opportunities to improve and get better. Stakeholders have to hold one another accountable through our actions, preparation, and execution of a common vision and mission of a plan that everyone owns and believes in. The work will be hard, and it will make you question yourself and your ability.

If your school is already on the right track, great! Stay the course. Let your initiatives and plan fully mature. Don't give up or change courses because you aren't seeing instant results. Don't throw that spaghetti against the wall! Trust the process, embrace the journey, and hang on for the long haul.

There is no greater feeling of accomplishment or fulfillment than when you are part of an effort that turns a school from failing to thriving. When you see hope restored, relationships take root, and opportunities soar, you know you're doing it right.

8

A NATIONALLY DISTINGUISHED STORY

The story of how Occoquan Elementary rose to become a Nationally Distinguished Title I School is one of hope, perseverance, and passion. Sports teams talk about winning championships. This is Occoquan's championship story. Every single person who lived this experience *owns* it. It's not just my story; it belongs to each stakeholder who poured his or her heart, soul, sweat, and tears into earning this award. We started it together, and we finished it together.

Four years into our journey of turning around Occoquan and reigniting the passion for teaching and learning—and a year before we earned the award—we began the process of application to be awarded the distinction as a Nationally Distinguished Title I School. When we reviewed the criteria, we discovered there had been a small change in meeting the submission requirements. We believed we had missed the mark by .5 percent. Half a percent! By that point, however, we were so driven to show the world what our school had done, we knew there was no stopping us. We had already pushed our individual and collective performance higher than anyone expected, but with just .5 percent between us and the win, we found another gear!

Any school can find success by incorporating the right systems, practices, and processes. Winning championships, however, is next-level living. It requires finding that extra gear—and fueling yourself, your team, and your students with passion, purpose, and drive. It demands that gang mentality—the willingness to do anything for your school family, to stand up for one another, and to beat the odds and overcome every obstacle, *together*. And that's what made Occoquan's five-year turnaround story and ultimate win so special. Beyond test results and awesome instruction, we were a family in every sense of the word. There was nothing we wouldn't do for each other. As a family, we went the extra mile for one another. If there was a funeral, we were all there. If someone was in need, we all showed up to help. We reminded one another often of our commitment by asking the question, "When you look over your shoulder, what do you see?" The answer was always, "Every single one of us, ready to go." We had each other's backs no matter what!

We Did It Our Way!

Mrs. Jenkins
second-grade teacher and team leader

August 2012, my entire world changed. How do I accept this radical man who has set a vision that was beyond what I had seen or imagined in my veteran years? How do you accept the vision of changing the mindset of teachers and children? You take a chance, and just do it! My colleagues and I developed a trust with Mr. Brewer that allowed us to flourish as educators. The vision was to do whatever was necessary to make our students connected, creative thinkers who were successful and passionate about learning. He instilled in us the belief that there was truly nothing we could not do. We believed that because he believed in us. When given the permission to do what we loved—we all became teaching superstars!

There is no school like Occoquan. Under Mr. Brewer's uniqueness, we came to school enthusiastic about our craft. We were truly a family. We all had so much fun building relationships with our students, parents, and peers. Our students began to feel the love from us and Mr. Brewer. He loved the students at Occoquan, and he loved us. They knew we cared about them. We invested our lives in our students. As the school began to change, students got engaged and wanted to be an integral part of their school's success. The love for learning was a go. The party began. Once all of our students were on board and the teachers were showing their crafts, success was just a day away. We worked hard but played even harder. Teaching never felt so good.

Mr. Brewer trusted us as teachers, and with that trust, we accepted the job of raising the bar for our school's education. He guided us as we took flight. From this journey, we became a school of excellence again, earning countless awards and welcoming visitors from various schools to see the "buzz at the O." One of our biggest rewards

was to win the honor of being the first school in the county to receive the Nationally Distinguished Title I School award! We traveled to Long Beach, California, to reap the benefits of our hard work. How proud we were to seize the moment! Our lives changed as we stood with our "Relentless Principal." I was so honored to be a part of the journey. We did it! We did it our way!

A huge thank you goes out to every single stakeholder from our school division, school board, teachers, parents, staff, community supporters, and to our most important stakeholders: *our students*! This chapter offers insight into some of the awesomeness that took place from 2012 to 2017. You may already be implementing some of the practices you'll read about here, and I think you may find some ideas and encouragement to help you take your school to the next level. Wherever you are in your journey, I hope what you read here will give you an opportunity to reflect on what you are doing and want to do.

THE BACKSTORY

Established in 1927, Occoquan Elementary is the oldest school in Prince William County, Virginia. The school is situated within an industrial urban setting on the eastern corridor of Route 1 and Interstate 95, backing onto the historical river district of Occoquan. (Under the building are trenches that lead to the World War II bunkers. It's super awesome to crawl under the school building and go explore.)

The Route 1 corridor is well known for its Title I schools and diverse communities that grapple with the hardships of poverty every day. In 2017, Occoquan Elementary was at 68 percent free and reduced lunch as a population and far exceeded the required 35 percent requirement to apply for the award. Over the years, we have fluctuated between 67 percent and 72 percent with so many more families living at or below the poverty line who do not qualify for additional financial assistance or aid.

What makes our community unique is that we have many minority parents and second-language families who have immigrated from all over the world. Our school represented cultures, countries, and religions from all corners of the world, and we were incredibly proud of our unique and diverse population of families. Together, we formed a magical collaboration and synergy of a village that had taken on the world to show that all children can learn, love, and celebrate their educational experience.

After many years of schools in our area receiving an honorable mention award, Occoquan Elementary was the very first Prince William County school to receive the designation as a Nationally Distinguished Title I School—an honor we could not have been more proud or humbled to receive.

As a community of teachers, students, families, and friends, we created a high-octane, high-achieving, caring, and nurturing educational environment. We believed that every child could learn, that everyone played a crucial role, that everyone was important, and that there was no room for excuses. We also celebrated regularly. From throwing concerts to black-light parties and dancing on tables and in the hallways, we got serious about creating exciting and authentic experiences for staff and children. These experiences and the environment we created changed the outcomes for our students and for families throughout our community. Our practices and initiatives were and still are viewed as innovative and cutting-edge and have become a model for elementary schools across the nation. In the years following the award, we received visitors almost daily who wanted to come and experience the magic! What we learned from it all is that when you make the focus your legacy and make your work about a calling to promote greatness for children, then there is nothing you cannot achieve.

THE RESULTS

We used data to drive our instruction as well as our professional development on a yearly, monthly, and weekly basis. We would mine and review not just state scores but also our very own data collections from quizzes and tests. It went deeper than glancing at pass-or-fail statistics; we pored over the data to find trends, patterns, and areas of weakness as well as strengths. Before each new school year, teachers would spend time in two to three meetings reviewing the question-by-question analysis of the previous year's scores in an effort to adjust pacing, planning, and techniques for the current year. Our policy was to look at individual data, not as an instrument to "hold teachers accountable" but to figure out how we could all be better for students. If one teacher was struggling, it meant we were all responsible for helping and supporting that teacher. We would figure out a plan to support and uplift each other. If a teacher was having success, we expected that that success be shared, unpacked, and understood so we could all impact all students.

Our data from this time tells a story of a school that moved in a direction of unprecedented growth. Through professional development, motivation, and a strong sense of community, the staff increased the scores of all students dramatically.

The data points during the time we were considered for the Nationally Distinguished title were an incredible example of closing the achievement gap. Our economically disadvantaged student pass rate in reading increased from a 59 percent to an 87 percent during those four years. In math, this group increased from a 79 percent to a 94 percent pass rate, topping the state average of 66 percent by 28 percentage points. Large areas of growth during this period included English language learners improving in reading by 32 percent and during this four-year period, we went from a pass rate of 62 percent to a pass rate of 86 percent and in math gaining 28 percent points in the four-year period going from 78 percent to a 94 percent for ESOL learners. Our greatest growth was seen in our students with disabilities, who increased their scores by 40 percent during this four-year period. They scored a pass rate of 52 percent in reading and climbed 20 percentage points to a pass rate of 72 percent, soaring well above the state average of 46 percent. The growth in math for special-education students during this four-year period was 51 percent and in the last year blossoming from a 62 percent pass rate to an 85 percent pass rate. This is a difference of 23 percentage points, and almost double the state average of 49 percent at the time.

Our overall data by grade after five years together finished like this (as presented on our school data profile at the time):

Grade	Year	Reading	Math	History	Science
3	2016–2017	89%	93%	-	-
	2012–2013	62%	70%	-	-
4	2016–2017	91%	94%	99%	-
	2012-2013	67%	72%	-	-
5	2016–2017	96%	96%	-	92%
	2012-2013	68%	71%	-	74%

In addition to this, we had pre-school-year data evaluation. Teachers met once a week during a schoolwide data meeting day to look at current summative and formative data in their PLCs. The data being reviewed included such things as end-of-unit tests, projects, running records, or observational data. Teachers analyzed this data looking for strengths and weaknesses in grades, classes, and students. Teachers looked at the percentage of their class that scored an 80 percent or higher rather than looking at class averages, unreliable data that is easily skewed by outliers. Looking at the percentage of students who received an 80 percent or higher gave a teacher a strong sense of mastery of standards. Teachers also looked at the pass rate of specific groups, including special-education and ESOL students, to ensure these groups were making adequate gains. Weekly lesson plans were then created around this data, and ideas were discussed for remediation. With the belief that no one student belonged to any one teacher, we all took responsibility for all the data, as a grade level, as a team, and as a school.

Our teachers took data seriously and used it as a tool for improvement and as a conversational piece. There is no shame around data, as it is all owned and evaluated in groups. Summative data was collected and posted onto Excel sheets and housed on a common drive so that it could be shared by teams as well as administrators and Title I support teachers. The Title I math and reading teachers were able to view and track students' performance on end-of-unit tests, offering support to classroom teachers, or pulling struggling students in groups for additional practice and remediation.

Data was not just kept within the walls of the school. Families were continuously kept up to date on student grades and progress. Grades were sent home on weekly reports, phone calls were made to celebrate student achievements, and student-led conferences were held. When needed, intervention meetings were held as a form of open dialogue between teachers, parents, and administrators. We implemented student-led parent conferences where the students would come with a prepared discussion, starting with a number of examples of what was going well and what their successes were. From there the students would share areas for growth and plans for improvement. We implemented this practice schoolwide (from K–5), and it proved incredibly successful. Because the students were facilitating the meetings, we would always have massive parent participation. We believed that data was the key to unlocking the potential inside of every student, and as such, should be viewed and shared by all those involved with that student.

INSTRUCTIONAL PRACTICES

In terms of the growth of our instructional practices, the gains made our starting place unrecognizable when compared to where we were five years in. We harnessed the awesomeness of our teachers by giving them the green light to make decisions as well as providing the support they needed to run uninhibited by archaic educational expectations, practices, and policies.

The key development started by ensuring that every single adult in the building was on the same page, walking to the same beat, sharing the same mission and vision. We implemented instructional practices that set the expectations in grades K–5. Some new practices would carve out success that would take time to materialize. It took a couple years, for example, to see the benefit of our implementation of a schoolwide expectation for handwriting. Just as we believed that a good writer is a good reader, we believed a good reader is a good writer. To enhance writing, we focused on the basic acquisition skill set of handwriting. The result was impressive, especially when you consider the minimal

The key development started by ensuring that every single adult in the building was on the same page, walking to the same beat, sharing the same mission and vision.

time investment of five to ten minutes we asked teachers to devote to a handwriting lesson. We found that, by focusing on the acquisition of basic skills such as reading, writing, and handwriting, literacy improves—which positively impacts every other area of instruction.

Schools have an obligation to support all learners and hold them to high expectations; it starts with an unwavering belief that all students can learn. We engaged our learning and instructional planning process to be data-driven so that there is a laser focus on all children. We developed inclusive processes and practices that remediate and enrich all students at all times from our day-to-day instructional practices, Saturday school, and after-school programs that combine study hall and STEAM programs.

Literacy

Reading instruction focuses on keeping it simple by ensuring children are reading, reading, reading. When you think of how much reading is going on in most schools every day, it is scary, especially the higher up we go. In the secondary setting, you can easily fall into the trap of delivering content not teaching content. I challenge you to follow a student around for a day or have teachers count the minutes in a day when students are reading. The feedback will be powerful.

We worked extremely hard to integrate reading and writing within all subjects every day. It became an expectation that teachers at every grade level would create relevant and authentic reading and writing experiences that continuously aligned with the curriculum and hit state learning objectives. Core literacy time had a K–5 alignment expectation; for example, a mini-lesson led into small-group guided instruction with research-based literacy stations. Within this structure, teachers had the flexibility to implement our programs in ways that they believed met the individual needs of their classroom. We started our reading groups on the first day of school, from kindergarten through fifth grade. Doing so ensured continuity across all our classrooms. Reading became part of the culture, and as students returned to school each year, they knew the expectations and routines from day one! We made sure that each classroom was outfitted with extensive classroom libraries that rotated each semester, ensuring every class had hundreds of books for selection by DRA, interest, and grade-level curriculum focus. In addition to this, we maintained a literacy center with a book room that housed thousands of books by DRA, reading strategy, chapter books, nonfiction, and fiction, as well as by curriculum.

One of the best ways our classroom teachers dealt with the needs of our diverse students was to differentiate instruction. The same structure for a mini-lesson and stations was applied across our content areas and through our small-group rotations during instruction. Kindergarten to fifth-grade teachers implement guided reading groups as a way to meet the needs of their students. These small groups are based upon student needs, and at times even extended outside the classroom if needed; for example, a fifth-grade teacher could have a reading group with two students from another fifth-grade classroom. These two were added to the group of four, rather than their teacher instructing them in a group of two. This allows one teacher to have a full group and the other to have more time to meet the needs of other readers. Instead of having outliers in each room, we aligned our schedules to be able to cross groups across the classrooms for direct instruction as needed. No one was left out; every student received the differentiated instruction they deserved.

In addition to small-group learning and teaching, we focused our reading and math programs for special groups of ESOL and SPED students by aiming to be as close to fully inclusive practices as possible. The expectation was that these students' instruction would be done through their core curriculum. This way large groups of children are not being removed from core instruction and experiences. Programs do not fix kids. Quality Tier One instruction from a teacher is the best, and our results supported this with some of the highest scores in ESOL and SPED in the state of Virginia.

Our school had a large English-learner (EL) population. Along with our school division, we made it a focus to provide professional development in this area. We made it a priority to be experts in the area of English learners. Each staff member had EL professional development yearly, as well as in-school implemented practice hours. Teachers were also asked to write and post language and curriculum objectives on their boards to draw attention to our focus for learning. Teachers became familiar with the standards for ESOL learners as prescribed by World-Class Instructional Design and Assessment (WIDA), as well as can-do descriptors for each of their students. This allowed them to have an extremely personal understanding of their ESOL students' capabilities and needs at that given time of their educational journey. All of these best practices and professional-development requirements led to an increased sensitivity and understanding of this large population as well as an increased ability to meet their needs.

Our teachers also embraced the open-door, open-classroom model of instruction, allowing for peer as well as administrative observations. Mentors and mentees, as well as full-teacher teams and visiting educators, observed classrooms in action seeking quality best practices and vertical alignment pieces. We were big fans of Instructional Rounds and would conduct these throughout the school year. This is an outstanding practice to help teachers observe and reflect on their own instructional practices and routines. Teachers enjoyed the opportunity to share and learn new ideas. Instructional Rounds also provided for vertical alignment that allowed teachers to understand what was taking place at the grades above and below them. I loved when a teacher would ask to go back and observe a colleague at a later date. We should always be celebrating and using the expertise inside our buildings and school divisions. Instructional Rounds are some of our most well-received professional development. I believe that, more often than not, the answer is already within our school. We just need to be sure that we are drawing upon the best practices and expertise of our amazing educators.

Math Instruction

As modeled in our reading instruction, our math instruction was also conducted in small groups, meeting students where they were in order to get them to where they needed to be for growth. We used (and still use) a blended mathematical approach, embracing several research-based philosophies and methods to deliver math instruction. We embraced the idea of basic acquisition of skills more so in math than in any other area. Students' ability to be able to perform and understand the basic concepts of math, math skills, and number sense sets them up for success in every subsequent level of math; for example, we took our students' ability to understand their basic facts seriously. We held basic facts quizzes and competitions like spelling bees, and the students loved it! Students learned to monitor their own progress and were able to grade themselves. We found students holding one another accountable as they set goals and worked together to achieve them.

Competition was a healthy component of our instruction, and while we foster collaboration, we also fostered healthy competition between classes and grades. The students thrived in this environment, and we tied it together with our motto of Four Tribes—One Village, which you will read about shortly.

The Magic of Hard Work and Love

Brian Slater
teacher/administrator

Interview day, August 2012, I rolled into Occoquan nervous and desperate for a job. Little did I know the journey I was about to be a part of over the next five years. I should have known it was going to be awesome, though, as Brewer wore a T-shirt, board shorts, and flip-flops while he and several of his teachers interviewed me in a kindergarten classroom. That was the first moment I knew I was in the right place!

Everything came together perfectly during that time! The perfect leadership, teamwork, and mentality. All of it forged together to make an unstoppable force. We were not going to be denied our opportunity to raise a championship banner at Occoquan. Our success during that time started with Brewer's leadership—focused, purposeful, and relentless. He pushed us to think outside the box with our instruction and gave us the green light when we had ideas. Our teamwork blossomed as we fed off each other's energy and ideas. We held each other accountable and didn't want to let one another down. The mentality of the school changed; excuses no longer had a place in our school. We were on a mission and did whatever was necessary for our students and each other.

Most leaders don't want staff cliques in their school, but Brewer had one that was called: "All-In for Students." No joke, the whole staff was eager and willing to join! The greatest part of this transformational journey was that it benefited our students and families. Brewer provided whatever resources we needed or wanted for our classrooms (To this day, I think he has a money tree hidden somewhere). It motivated us to pour every single last piece of energy we had into our students each day. They experienced educational

moments that they'll remember forever because of that. Our families were welcomed with open arms and given the sense of comfort knowing their child would be nurtured and loved unconditionally. It was no fluke that we won Nationally Distinguished; Occoquan was a magical place built on hard work, commitment, and love.

I owe who I am today as an educator and leader to Brewer. He never let me settle for being average and always pushed me to get better. He taught me the importance of surrounding yourself with quality people who are hungry for more. To this day, he is my mentor and I'm forever grateful for that.

Grades K–2 utilized Assessing Math Concepts Assessments (AMC), a series of pre- and post-assessments that teachers conducted with students one on one. These assessments determined what a student knew and what they still needed to learn. Based on student responses to interview-type questions on counting and number sense, AMC provides teachers with a list of specific activities from the Developing Number Concepts text that will support students with what they still need to learn. We were able to use this information to group students based on ability for differentiation and remediation. Teachers and support staff used recommended activities from Developing Number Concepts for teacher-directed instruction and independent student practice. Post-assessments consistently show growth in our students' number sense. We made sure throughout our grade levels that math instruction was tied to authentic, relevant, and real learning experiences. It would not be uncommon to find a math lesson taking place through a restaurant, developing a business, or maintaining a bank account. We were always coming up with unique ideas for instruction that mirrored something from the real world.

In our upper grades, students were pre-assessed using teacher-created tests before beginning new units. Teachers used the data from these tests to group students according to their knowledge and readiness for the subject area. Within these groups, students were taught problem-solving skills as well as computational strategies. Students and teachers utilized methods such as the Bar method: "Understand, Plan, Solve, and Check problem-solving," partial product and sum, and algorithms. We again made math incredibly fun through authentic, relevant, and real learning experiences.

Another way we reinforced our reading, writing, and cross-curriculum connections was through our grades K–5 expectation to start every math lesson with a math problem of the day. These problems were geared toward higher-level thinking and often involved multiple-step problems. Our students had been struggling with multistep word problems, and this became a solution to help students engage in this area of difficulty every day. The students would show their work on whiteboards so the teacher could easily observe and assess the students together in a timely manner. Students completed the problems on their own, then worked through them as a class. Data was collected and monitored to observe student as well as class growth.

Students at Occoquan were afforded many opportunities for increasing their academic abilities as well as their areas of interest. Grades 3–5 were offered free after-school STEAM programs, where students spent an hour in study hall getting academic assistance before moving on to an hour of a STEAM activity of their choice. These activities ranged from art and photography to journalism and debate, to Battle of the Books. Every year, students looked forward to the start of this program with enthusiasm, and they knew that everything was earned. To attend, they had to complete an hour of study hall. What was awesome is that we were able to increase our school day with this program, ensure that all our students came to remediation, and we didn't run into homework issues because the students could complete homework during this time!

Occoquan Tribes

Ever since I was a boy at school, I had been involved with some form of house system. I was even a House Captain in high school, and as I've moved from school to school, I have helped implement a version of a house system. House systems have become popular again in recent years because of movies like the *Harry Potter* series and the outstanding example set by the Ron Clark Academy.

When I first arrived at Occoquan, I wanted to implement a house system once again; however, at the time we were not ready. The conditions were right, and the scenario of being Occoquan: Home of the Braves could not have been more perfect as the theme would move from house system to a tribal system. We just weren't there in terms of our culture and being all-in. A huge mistake that schools make when it comes to implementing new concepts and ideas is that they jump right in without buy-in or support from their stakeholders. When that happens, good ideas can die a slow, painful death. Over the summer, after putting every student into a tribe and aligning the entire school, with the help of our steward, school secretary Anna Linton, we decided to shelve the idea until further notice.

That being said, once we were ready to roll, it would be hard to argue against the tribal system becoming one of the greatest contributing factors to the success of our school as it helped us truly embrace and bring out the power of family and community presence in our school—a school where everybody is somebody.

Occoquan became a school staffed by those willing to go the extra mile, those who built a family within the walls of the school, and those who believed they have a mission and not a job. This sense of family and presence has filled the halls of the school and was given form through the creation of four tribes that form our one Occoquan family. "Four Tribes—One Family!"

The tribal system was born from me as the leader leaving my ego at the door and realizing that by embracing those around me and creating leadership opportunities for everyone, great things would happen. Strength in numbers! We would form a teacher-leadership group in an airport after professional development to tackle a couple of core school issues—parent, student, and community engagement, student behavior, or instructional focus. As principal, I was super proud to empower teacher ownership and leadership in a core school initiative that completely changed the culture and expectation at Occoquan. We developed a process and worked through a systematic process to completely overhaul our school through our tribal system. Every piece of the program was carefully thought about and planned. It was a system where every student and staffer in the school was placed into one of four tribes. Kindergarten students now have connections to fifth-grade teachers, custodians, and office workers as they proudly bond over tribes.

In keeping with our tribal theme, the tribe names came from native languages from four of the many continents that represented our diverse population, while the meaning of the tribal names came from the leadership pillars of the United States Marines Corps whom, as a staff, we had spent time studying. There was *Mpango*, meaning initiative, *Altruista*, meaning unselfishness, *Lealtad*, meaning loyalty, and *Seigo-Sei*, meaning integrity. The traits of these tribes were followed and modeled not only by tribal members but the entire school because we were four tribes—one family. Every student received a free tribal T-shirt, and special ceremonies took place for tribal announcements and for new tribal members. The school celebrations had become famous nationwide with people from boards of supervisors, superintendents, and teachers from all over the state wanting to participate. New students would be welcomed into our school with a spin of the tribal wheel, built by a parent and hung in our front office, and with one magical spin and a crowd going crazy in hope the new student would be selected to their tribe.

These tribes have been an amazing success as they built a further sense of family and pride in our school. Everything in our school had been influenced by our tribal program, from instructional groups to celebrations and the walls of our school. Nothing moved without it being about and through the tribal experience! This helped create a school culture and camaraderie that was second to none. This success taught our students about ownership and accountability, respectful healthy competition, and the power of teamwork, which contributed to great decreases in student behavior problems. In the classroom, teachers used the tribal system as a behavior system focused on positive behaviors. Students would often work and sit in their tribes, and they love this sense of community, competition, and pride! No longer did teachers have to focus on negative behavior or reactionary response to student behavior, participation, or engagement.

The magic spilled over into our student homes, with many families posting on social media pictures of their support of their tribe, even to the extent that they would share this in later years with our school board! Parents and teachers would wear their tribe swag proudly, and we would count down weeks of anticipation to find our tribe champions for the year. It became a huge honor to be selected to become a tribal leader. I was most proud of the fact that our Native American families were truly proud of how we had embraced the Native American culture in such an honorable way supporting it, learning about it, and ensuring respect and honor for years to come.

The tribes successfully met and exceeded all expectations from the entire school staff and community. It had a transformational effect on everything possibly associated to our school from engagement to behavior, instruction, and student achievement. Our tribal system furthered our school's vocabulary as we taught our students to chase 100, to be relentless in all they do, and to take pride in themselves as they strive to become better individuals.

1:1 Take Home Tablet Program

As a school, we had been investigating 1:1 device programs that various schools and school divisions had implemented over the years. We found many to have had varying degrees of success. What we had found was that the implementation of a 1:1 program was like a shiny new toy, an idea that sounded sexy and was a feel-good program that lacked actual impact on student achievement. Most programs we found were limited to access at school and focused on pockets of student groups for use. Not to mention that 1:1 programs were incredibly difficult to get off the ground for start-up and ongoing funding.

As principal, my goal had always been to ensure all children had an opportunity to participate in the best instructional practices that education could offer. The vision for our 1:1 tablet program was to extend the school day through access to the student's online intervention programs, changing how we looked at homework, and providing an effective station at math and literacy time. We didn't want students to have individualized tablets without a purpose and focus. It was this program and the acquisition of our tablets that helped to have a significant impact on our results, scores, and earning the Nationally Distinguished award. We strongly believed that technology *enhanced* instruction; it didn't drive instruction. It extended the school day and the reach of our instructional practices into the home.

To successfully bring our vision to reality, we had to tackle a number of key issues including budgeting for purchases, selecting the right tablet, operating within the school division's current policies and practices, offering teacher and student professional development, devising a plan for in-home internet access, and figuring out what programs would and would not work on the devices we selected. In every sense, the 1:1 program was a significant undertaking that needed to be done well if it was to be successful.

In the early stages of our implementation, we were able to supply tablets to some individual classes through purchasing from school funds. After seeing how excited our students and teachers were to participate in the 1:1 device program, we began to look for creative ways to accelerate it. We were fortunate enough to be able to partner with some local business leaders who saw value in the initiative and wanted to impact our minority and diverse student population as a Title I school. In a few short months, we quickly had a device for an entire grade level. We elected to start with the third grade, as we wanted the tablets to travel with students from year to year, and even though it would have been easier to put the tablets in the hands of our fifth graders, we elected to build from the foundation up.

A New Family

Kerri Cabacar
educational leader/science teacher

It started at an airport bar with a few sketches on some cocktail napkins, that feeling of freedom and support. I'd been teaching for eight years, in three different schools, under four different administrators, and I'd never felt so excited to be a part of something. With a group of other teachers, I was part of building a tribal system from the ground up. The colors, the names, the symbols—each was picked with purpose. We were given the keys and told to drive it like we stole it! Over the course of a week, we put together the structure, with only one rule from Brewer: families had to stay together. Not a surprising rule considering his belief that family comes first. To this day, this undertaking remains the highlight of my career and my proudest legacy. In the development of the tribal system, I saw my first glimpses of the real leadership abilities of Hamish. This would be one of the first big changes for that elementary school, and it was going to be monumental; yet, he was not at the forefront. In fact, the day we launched the entire system to the staff, he had to be out of the building. But he didn't stop us; instead, he empowered us to be the change. He put into action one of his biggest beliefs: Give your staff the tools they need, and they will amaze you. I am truly honored to have been a teacher given the tools and the push I needed to succeed.

What has made our 1:1 program unique and successful has been our solution to internet access in the home. We applied for a Sprint Grant, and to our surprise, we won. When you run the numbers, the free internet access through the grant added up to what we believed to be about $1.5 million and gave almost unlimited internet access to 350 hotspots over a four-year period. This enabled us to be able to provide 350 individualized hotspots for our children to personally access the internet anywhere in the United States. It was a game changer for us—and it launched our next set of challenges around school division policies, practices, and capabilities such as network loads and internet access inside the building.

Within the first year, we were able to supply more than 100 individualized tablets and hotspots to the entire third grade. By the end of the second year, we had supplied the next grade level of children, and we made it a priority to ensure that every ESOL and SPED student had a hotspot and tablet. After extending the capacity of the tablets and hotspots in use to over 300 students being impacted daily and knowing that they retained their tablets for a three-year period, we have introduced Amazon Kindles to our kindergarten through second grade as a way to implement and extend our program into our younger grade levels.

As a result of our implementation of our tablets and hotspots, we were able to meet and exceed our original goals and vision for our 1:1 program, which positively impacted our schoolwide instruction, student engagement, and student achievement. We were also excited about how it had transformed what homework looked and felt like for our students. Homework would no longer be a grind; students were participating beyond programs and using tablets for research and presentation.

Almost all of our homework was done via the web. We no longer had parent complaints about homework. Students were engaged and motivated by their experience, and we had students working on areas of need through the research-based intervention programs online. We were able to monitor student usage of the tablets and the programs they were using, and the intervention programs provided real-time data updates on student progress. So this data acted as a secondary point we could use to gauge student progress and cross-reference against the work our teachers were doing. Let me be clear: Programs don't fix kids; it's amazing teachers who make the difference!

Virginia Tech Kindergarten to College Program

We had the good fortune to partner with Virginia Polytechnic Institute and State University and participate in their amazing Kindergarten to College program. This program is geared toward fifth graders from high-needs schools in the Virginia Tech local area, and we were the only school outside of Blacksburg at the time participating in this program.

The trips to Virginia Tech were a huge success and a magical experience for the fifth-grade students who got to attend—it was considered a rite of passage! The trips offered students an opportunity to set foot on a college campus for an entire day and participate in class with students. Being a school with a high poverty and diverse second-language population, for 95 percent of our students, this was the first and only time that many of them would ever be afforded the opportunity to set foot on a college campus until much later in life. The good news for our students is they got the opportunity to truly visualize and feel that their dream could become a reality because of this experience.

Prior to the students' visit, a Virginia Tech team of professors and teachers came to our school and conducted pre-visits, where surveys were filled out and presentations were given about campus life and opportunities at Tech, including the expectations around how their visit would go. We had our students prepare for the visit by studying every fact, sound, and piece of information they could get their hands on. We wanted our students to be content experts whenever they took a field trip of any kind. This was an expectation. Once they had studied for the field trip, they could then take a quick quiz, and they were expected to score a 90 percent or higher on it to attend. Again, this ensured that their trip was an amazing experience because they had the knowledge to truly appreciate and enjoy it.

Each year we have funded the entire trip to ensure that no student misses out. The students arrive at school by four a.m. to hop on a coach that has us arriving at Tech by nine a.m. As a result of this Virginia Tech partnership, we were able to expand our business partnership to include D.C. Trails, a bus service that now provides us discounted rates on all trips for us because they wanted to be involved in the vision of the program, and it was an opportunity for them to give back to their community.

Side note: It is important to reach out to your community and business partners. They want to help! The trick is to not sell them a dream; sell them a reality. When dealing with your local community business partners, you need to think like a business owner, not an educator. Business operators that are successful deal in reality; they have a plan, take action, and work with focus. When meeting with potential partners, come to the table with a plan not just an idea or dream. Show them what has already been done and what you can do with their help.

Upon arrival, the university greeted us at the bus, where our students would perform the Virginia Tech chants each year. Virginia Tech pulls out all the stops starting with the provost greeting all the students, after which the students break into small groups and attend classes. Over the years, our students have been vet students, engineer and space engineering students, and have participated in 3D laser imaging, robotics, and space science, to name a few. One of the highlights for the students every year is having the opportunity to eat with the Virginia Tech Cadets and students in the cafeterias. I think we ran the buffet and ice-cream machines dry!

The students complete the trip by working with the student-athletes and visiting the sports stadiums at Virginia Tech. The highlight was that the students (and adults, for that matter) get to run out through the tunnel and out onto the football field at Tech, jumping up and touching the Hokie Stone as they go! What I really enjoy is the Q & A session with the student-athletes. It puts into perspective for the students the reality of participating in college life as a student-athlete. The message is always "student first, athlete second" which is a powerful message for our students, who all think they are going to college to play sports.

On the return home, we see a profound change take place. After this trip, it's like our students grow up overnight. They set new goals, talk about going to college, and work harder to do well on their exams and daily assignments. It is truly a transformational experience for the students. There is not a school that should not be doing this. I believe all schools should be providing this experience to their children. Take it as a challenge: Find a college that would like to partner with your school, and make it happen!

INNOVATIVE PROFESSIONAL DEVELOPMENT

It has always been a mission of mine to provide the very best professional-development program to all the employees at my schools. I have had the vision to turn professional development upside down and to look outside the box, much like the business and innovative leaders from organizations such as Google, Apple, and Amazon.

I want to focus my lenses for educators through innovators like Steve Jobs, Richard Branson, and Elon Musk. My goal is to make professional development vibrant, relevant, and authentic. I want my teachers and employees, as result of what they learn, to push boundaries and work to become better not only as professionals but personally as well.

The professional development we did at Occoquan defies typical professional development as it breaks through barriers and state lines. The staff at Occoquan was able to partake in team-building professional development and curriculum-related learning that far exceed the norm of educators. Teachers and employees at our school have contributed to the ownership and direction of professional development that helped inspire significant gains in student achievement, instructional practices, and out-of-the-box thinking.

All too often, teachers are told what to focus on rather than asked what they would like to focus on. That's why at the beginning of the year, each educator in our school develops an individualized professional-growth plan. These plans draw on data to show areas of growth and need, and they include the teacher's personal-passion projects. Our goal is to encourage and enable teachers to chase a personal-passion project that they want to pursue. As we're able to do so, we provide the funds and resources to make this happen. The results have been incredible not only for the adults in the school but also the students and wider community as was evident through our teacher "Act of Kindness" program we developed one year. Teachers found professional development to truly be that—professional and even personal *development*. Our plan was not to be out to get teachers. Our plan was to grow teachers and help them become the most amazing educators they could be. When you do this, not only do the educators and school win, but most importantly, the students win!

At the beginning of the school year, upon the teachers' return for the first day back at school, we have always taken a trip somewhere to enhance the curriculum, to conduct team building, staff meetings, and have summer book reviews. It also provides another opportunity to celebrate and reflect on the amazing work we do as educators. The funny thing about taking a trip the first day is that we ended up spending more time focused on the topics we wanted to, and we got more focused face time with our educators than we ever would sitting in a room somewhere at school. All too often, schools focus on coming back and spending the first day looking at rules, regulations, and data. This is information that highly engaged professionals should already know, and you end up spending time demoralizing your team. If you are having to revisit this information regularly, your staff is not fully engaged in the educational process, and I think you have bigger problems! Instead you should be embracing the very few and far between opportunities to bring your entire staff together to motivate, model, build relationships, focusing on the vision and mission of the school. and preparing to knock it out for your students!

The first day is often a missed opportunity, wasted on bad professional development and doing all the things we tell teachers not to do in their classrooms with kids. To make better use of this initial time together, for the past few years, we have taken our entire staff on field trips to Washington, D.C., the United States Marine Corps, New York City, and Philadelphia.

Again, we paid for this through business partnerships, and we didn't waste money on T-shirts or gimmicky gifts. We wanted to model the expectation around authentic and relevant learning experiences.

Our trip to Philadelphia, for example, provided us the opportunity for professional development that included not only learning and reviewing the roots of our country but also building and developing our grade-level teams' curriculum knowledge. A photo scavenger hunt led us through the history-rich streets as teams took pictures in unique places. The joy and the bonding of this day led to natural conversation about teaming, expectations, and hopes for the new school year. Plus who doesn't like a Philly cheesesteak?! Our trip to New York took us to the Statue of Liberty and up through the 9/11 Memorial. We held a staff meeting in Central Park and then headed to Times Square. Those learning experiences are priceless. Not once did anyone refuse to go. Everyone was all-in, and they felt valued and respected as professionals, as they should be.

Some of our most well-received professional development comes from our own in-house resources. I believe that, more often than not, the answer is in the room. We just need to be sure that we are drawing upon the best practices and expertise of our amazing educators.

Other professional development provided over the years has included trips to places like the famed Ron Clark Academy and conferences across the country that teachers found, which aligned to their learning and curriculum. No experience would be spared or wasted. We would bring professionals and experts into our school for work sessions in small groups, by grade levels and in content areas. I always felt it was important to set our specialists up as coaches, not just extra hands to take small groups. They are content experts for a reason, and we utilize this knowledge to provide professional development in content areas such as reading and math, or even PE.

Family Always Comes First

Kelly Friedman
teacher assistant

As a teacher's assistant at Occoquan Elementary School, I had the honor and privilege to work with Mr. Brewer and have him become part of my family. When Mr. Brewer took over as principal of Occoquan Elementary in 2012, of course I was a little nervous—nervous about what to expect and the changes that we would go through. Two months into the school year, Hurricane Sandy destroyed my parents' house in Brooklyn, New York. I needed to take the time to assist my family but didn't want to seem like an employee who was never at work. My fears could not have been more misplaced. When I shared my situation with Mr. Brewer, he immediately told me to take all the time I needed; family always comes first. As I was helping my family in New York, without my knowledge, Mr. Brewer was organizing donations from the Occoquan staff. These donations helped my family and many others in Brooklyn during a time of need.

I have so many examples of how Mr. Brewer has impacted my life and family. One of the most amazing examples is when he created an opportunity for my daughter who has special needs to volunteer at Occoquan Elementary. Mr. Brewer gave her a purpose and place to belong. In 2015, after my son graduated from college as a special-education teacher, he accepted a position at Occoquan Elementary. Knowing that Mr. Brewer would take care of him and give the green light to create the best opportunities for all students was exciting.

Finally, the greatest lesson I learned from Mr. Brewer was to always be all-in for kids, no matter what it takes. Mr. Brewer would say, "Sweep the sheds. It doesn't matter what your title or position is, your place is important in the lives of all students."

Mr. Brewer, thank you for leaving me better than you found me. I know when I look over my shoulder who will be there.

I have always had a love of the military and both the leadership and teamwork that take place there. It has not been uncommon for me to invite in current or retired military and special forces personnel to talk to my staff about their personal experiences with teamwork and leadership. And it is always well received.

We live in a day and age when safety is a top concern of staff, and rightly so! We prepare for the safety of our children, staff, and building with the same rigor and expectation of delivering our instruction. We don't have a moment to lose, and we want to be prepared and make it count! We have been fortunate enough through my association with Principal Andy Jacks to partner with the Washington, D.C. SWAT teams for professional development on crises—active-shooter scenarios, for example. The opportunity completely changed our practices as a result, and we have worked on scenarios to ensure our staff were highly trained and ready. Through this training, we learned a lot about our building, how to operate in an emergency, and what may or may not happen in a particular emergency. Most importantly, we've learned how to respond more appropriately and effectively.

I highly encourage you to reach out and work with your local emergency services. What I learned is that they would accept an invitation to work with you, your staff, and in your schools with open arms! Do not wait, and do not hesitate. No regrets!

FACILITY AND INFRASTRUCTURE INITIATIVES

Over the years, one of my most favorite things to do as an educator or principal is to enhance the classroom or building with everything from upgrades to cleanup, repurposing, technology, paint, lights, you name it! The things in and around your building are an opportunity to enhance the learning potential and experiences for your students and families. I find facility management to be one of the most exciting aspects of the job, and I've come to understand an opportunity to make some of the biggest impacts on all our stakeholders. If you are not considering the opportunity you have in the area of facility management, you are missing out!

Space

We are still building schools with an archaic layout from distant years past. While building square boxes is cost-effective and neutral, our students live in a world that is not a square box. I am passionate about making our environments and instruction a reflection of the world that students are graduating into—a world that is diverse and creative. When you go into an Apple Store, for example, they play on your senses to lure you in and to engage you in their products and vision. Organizations like this want you to have an experience. They want you to feel good and leave feeling like you became part of their vision and experience. Another great example is Chick-fil-A. This company ensures you feel like a million dollars, from the greetings like "thank you" and "my pleasure," to the cleanliness of its restaurants. I have been so impressed with the customer service of this organization that I paid for my entire office staff to have lunch there for professional development to observe their workings and interactions with their customers and stakeholders.

Sound

The senses play into every aspect of human engagement—sight, touch, smell, sound—and facility management should correlate to these senses.

As the concept and my work grew around exploring the human sensors of education, I was lucky enough to meet a recent college graduate, Lucas Goss, who was doing some research and program work in this area, with a focus on the impact of sound in the classroom, including the use of audio-enhanced voice projection systems. As leaders, we cannot be afraid to engage our stakeholders and resources around us, and for me, Lucas was certainly one of the most talented young individuals with whom I have had the opportunity to collaborate. His work was introduced to me as he was substituting at our school. When I started exploring audio-enhanced systems to put in the classroom, I discovered a wide spectrum of features and cost. Lucas helped me evaluate the options for audio-enhanced voice projection systems, and once we had settled on a product and began purchasing, he helped us implement the use of the systems in classrooms.

I was blown away by how receptive teachers were to the systems. As word spread throughout the building, they signed up for the chance to use them. What started out as a fifth-grade implementation quickly turned into ensuring every single class had them. Our results from using our systems show that teachers' voices were protected, meaning healthy educators with decreased time out of school. The 360-degree sound and pitch reached students' sensors at different levels of engagement and focus, plus you could mute the system during small group, or turn it up to hear whole-word pronunciation, something that is helpful for English learners.

The bonus was that we had a cord that connected to our interactive boards. We immediately upgraded those as well, and finally, students used the system during their own classroom facilitation and presentations.

Music!

We wanted to impact the experience students were having in the hallways. We saw the entire building as an opportunity to impact learning, and we looked at our walls, ceiling, and corridors as an extension of the classroom. A great example of this was our introduction of sound in the hallways; we had installed a speaker system in the hallways whereby music could be played throughout the day. Before school, we played fun music, and as kids entered the building, their sense of engagement and excitement would rise, and they would be actively ready for the day. It was not unusual to see students dancing and skipping in the hallways to the music. With today's apps for music, it is very easy to find and play the music you want for free or at a small cost. We were the Home of the Braves and embraced our Native American culture, so during the school day as students were engaged in their learning process or moving about the building, we played Native American music that proved to be incredibly calming and relaxing for not just the students but the faculty as well.

Lighting

Schools spend too much time under bad, yellow light. This dull light is unengaging, like a wet, rainy day inside your building. Students become sluggish and sleepy under these lights. I know some educators love the idea of teaching with the lights off, and while there is a time and place for that, instruction should not take place in a dark or dull room. Looking back, I am so glad that I took a chance to do my own little test in my school. I worked with a teacher to have all their lights in the classroom replaced with daylight bulbs to see what would happen with engagement and student work production—it was astonishing the impact. Students were more active, vibrant, alert, and engaged in their educational process. As a result of this, we decided to implement the process of replacing every light bulb in our building with an upgrade to daylight bulbs.

Seating

To help differentiate and enrich our instructional processes, we removed and replaced our desks with tables. The new tables offered an opportunity for students to collectively collaborate and communicate with each other in a space that was conducive to productive activity. Again the tables were visually stimulating to the environment because we were able to get them in bright colors and shapes.

There has been a real movement around getting students moving and having more time to play. As a teacher, I was always working on ways to have students moving around, and I would always be sneaking them out for extra recess because the students needed it and *I* needed it. Instead of brain breaks that regularly felt like a waste of time, I would prefer to have them go run around, even if the weather wasn't the best—a short run around the courts was always better than nothing. So as a staff, we started chatting about the idea of trialing a second recess, and very quickly the idea caught on, and teachers were noticing a substantial difference in the engagement and activity of the students in the room. As staff, we discussed going schoolwide, and we agreed as a collective that we would move to double recess. The staff helped iron out a schedule and ensured each grade level got out at the best times.

Other Initiatives

The ambassador program is a unique program to Occoquan, focusing on the development of English language learners and instilling in them leadership qualities as well as pride for their culture. This group was granted the opportunity to travel to the United States Embassy in full cultural regalia for a genuine experience.

In addition to all the programs offered before and after school, we offered unlimited field trips whereby grade-level teams planned field trips to museums, zoos, national monuments, and in-house presentations such as corn husking, reptile houses, and historical collections. Our students should be getting authentic learning experiences, and there is no better opportunity for this than putting students on location. When you look around your community, you begin to see all the opportunities that are out there for educators to bring learning alive through a hands-on experience. Do not pass up the opportunity to put kids on location. When the learning is real and tangible, the students engage in the process.

I'll never forget the day we began trialing double recesses. We presented the idea to the team after joking around about it and we decided, "Let's get serious about it and give the idea of a double recess some thought." A few teachers tried it for their classes, and the results were almost instant. We found students were more engaged, settled, and focused on their learning experience, and behavior issues decreased. Seeing the success and results, we decided collectively to make it a schoolwide expectation that our students had two recesses. As for the obvious questions of how to make time for two recesses, we found that we actually ended up saving time. Students were quicker to respond, we were not losing time to behavioral disruptions and slow transitions, and we weren't wasting time with gimmicky brain breaks.

COMMUNITY ENGAGEMENT

The staff at Occoquan worked with the belief that it takes a team to support and strengthen a student. Parents and family members are important parts of this team. To help parents build confidence and feel a part of their child's school life, Occoquan had several programs and support teams in place. Social media practices and sharing of information and instructional practices opened up to a live feed of the operations of the school to families as well as the community. We used Facebook and Twitter accounts, and the hashtag #o_braves, to enable parents and community members to see the day-to-day work of students and teachers in real time.

In order to meet our population's needs and to make them feel comfortable as a part of their child's education, teachers created English classes for parents offered at night in the school. We made them free to ensure everyone could come. We opened them to participants being able to bring extended family members and friends. The families were able to bring their children, and we would provide babysitting. Our staff also supports the Parents as Educational Partners program that highlights school practices and programs for parents in small group-led classes.

Movie nights, math and literacy programs, and family fun fairs are other ways parents were welcomed into the Occoquan culture. The most enjoyed event, multicultural night, invites parents and community members to come and celebrate their culture through food, fashion, dance, and celebration.

Occoquan had many school–community partnerships designed to improve student achievements. For example, a local church donated filled backpacks every September for students who could not afford supplies. A Spanish radio station donated airtime to advertise for the English classes held at the school and provided free of charge to Spanish-speaking adults. The Spanish Foundation of America donated money for the purchase of laptops, and Patient First donated $1,000 a year for the purchase of new chapter books. Youth for Tomorrow, a program that works with schools in northern Virginia, offered a variety of programs to our children and families in need and in crisis to support the Occoquan family.

We worked hard to give opportunities to all students, including those with disabilities. We wanted to plant seeds that would grow as they do, creating a stronger future for each of them.

Therefore, we created a community-based instruction program to benefit our students with disabilities, putting these students into their communities to practice functional and social skills. In most counties, students in secondary grades are the ones granted this opportunity. As a school, we wanted to focus on basic social and functional needs of our exceptional learners at the elementary level, empowering these young children.

Fathers were welcomed into the school with our WATCH Dogs program. Girl Scout troops had taken over our school's gardens, and local businesses supported us with donations when and where possible. The community involvement was made evident through our yearly satisfaction surveys that we experienced near perfection with close to 100 percent satisfaction.

This was just a little insight to the enormous work that went on during a four- and five-year period to take on the task of getting our little elementary school recognized as one of the highest-performing schools. As a community, we proved that you can do almost anything when you put your heart, mind, and soul into it and you believe in each other and every single child. We believed, and our belief took us all the way to a Nationally Distinguished Title I School Award. My hope is that you can draw some inspiration and support from our work and apply some things that might help propel your school forward and ensure all students are winning.

Occoquan's Camelot

Mrs. Ferrara
teacher

What a magical time the years from 2012–2017 were at Occoquan Elementary School! I refer to this memorable time as "Occoquan's Camelot" because, according to the Merriam-Webster dictionary definition, Camelot is "a time, place, or atmosphere of enjoyable happiness."

I truly witnessed Occoquan's atmosphere change most favorably beginning in August 2012, when Hamish Brewer began his first year as our principal. Even when I first met Mr. Brewer in May 2012, I knew he was unique. Of course, I enjoyed listening to his New Zealand accent; however, he possessed certain attributes which no other principal I worked for had: such a high-spirited personality and the desire to always remember that our number-one goal was our children at the "O."

Wow! My intuition was correct. Throughout Mr. Brewer's time at Occoquan, he inspired so many people, and provided the "O" with an extremely enjoyable, energetic atmosphere for learning, and for having *fun*! There wasn't a day that went by that Mr. Brewer didn't tell and show the children and staff that he loved them. One could feel Mr. Brewer's enthusiasm within the walls and halls of Occoquan. He gave courage to everyone!! Even as a veteran teacher, he gave me the courage and confidence to conquer any new technology program! He continuously motivated me to reach new heights as a teacher. His leadership provided the staff and the children the feeling that we could do the impossible, or what others thought was the impossible, for our children. We proved that we could—and we *did* by earning the National Distinguished Title I Award in 2016!

During Occoquan's Camelot years, Mr. Brewer and I not only developed a sound professional relationship, but we also formed a very special bond almost like a mother-to-son relationship. In fact, my own son often had conversations with Mr. Brewer asking for brotherly advice. On many occasions, Mr. Brewer and I had several chats about him taking better care of his health, continuing to love his wonderful family to the fullest, remembering where he came from, as well as talking about my family and their challenges. Whenever we ended our conversations, our common thread was how Occoquan was definitely a Camelot because of his amazing, relentless leadership!

One of the saddest days of my educational career occurred in May 2017, when Mr. Brewer informed me he was going to take over the principalship of Fred Lynn Middle School.

Fighting back my tears, I knew that starting in August 2017, Fred Lynn was soon on its way of developing its own Camelot because of the qualities Mr. Brewer would share with their children and staff.

9

RELENTLESS AND THE FRED LYNN STORY

On July 12, 2013, education activist Malala Yousafzai addressed the United Nations Youth Assembly in New York and gave a thought-provoking speech in which she said, "One child, one teacher, one book, and one pen can change the world." We go to work to inspire and be the difference for our students, schools, and communities. Having dedicated my entire career to working with students and communities of poverty and Title I schools, never before has this work been more important than right now. Our schools are that one place where we can have hope to inspire and change the world one student at a time.

My whole life, I have been drawn to the helping the under-dog, the underestimated; I tend to side with those who rise up and come from behind to ultimately stand tall, achieve, and win. This latest chapter in my life would be no different. And with my love for educators like Joe Clark and Coach Carter, I wanted into that club, that legacy!

After I had interviewed and been selected as the principal at Fred Lynn Middle School, the reaction was swift and surprising. For some it made sense, and for others it did not. A number of people asked me the same question about my leaving my previous school. They would all ask why you would give up one of the best elementary schools in the state of Virginia and the country after all the hard work. We had only just received a designation of Nationally Distinguished Title I School. My answer has and will not change: You have to be a person of conviction and stand up for what you believe is right. While I saw Fred Lynn struggling for years and had heard and read all the stories, it frustrated me that in my community we couldn't find an answer, and it seemed from an outsider's perspective to only be getting worse. It was my opinion that I could not stand idle any longer, that I had to put my name in the hat for consideration because who am I if I don't put my hand up? If I didn't go for it, I felt that I would be taking the easy option. We find out who we are when no one is watching, when the difficult decisions have to made. This is the true quest for legacy!

Fred Lynn had a long history of underperformance and its fair share of failures. To some, it was considered one of the toughest schools in the state of Virginia. Much of what had been said or written about the school was close to being true or had elements of truth to it, and you only need to read the reviews and messages left online by the public, students, and parents to get an understanding of how difficult things had become. The school's population was made up of diverse, high-poverty, second-language-speaking students.

Approximately 88 percent qualified for free or reduced-priced lunches, and many of the families that didn't qualify lived right on the poverty line.

The school had struggled with poor academic performance, underachievement, high staff turnover, student discipline, and instructional issues for years, and it seemed that for every step forward, two more would be taken back. The staff that remained were and are committed to helping, supporting, and uplifting children and improving the school. Although there had been some small signs of improvement, it wasn't enough to move the dial, and it wasn't for a lack of trying, fight, or commitment. Most often in difficult times, educators can be left focusing on the wrong things or spinning their wheels on what others think the focus ought to be. Also, it was just a simple fact that their story was being told by someone else other than themselves. When you leave your story to be told by someone else, you leave it open to interpretation by others, and the power is in the holder of the pen.

While I was transitioning from Occoquan to Fred Lynn, I had been introduced to the team from FreeThink Media, who had reached out to me to discuss possibly documenting my work. FreeThink is a media-production house that tells stories about our changing world, for people who want and are having a hand in changing it. They had done some amazing stories over the years on cutting-edge ideas, technology, and people. For some reason, they thought I was doing something interesting enough to tell the world about it. They had found me through a *Washington Post* article that was headlined, "Tribal Wars Meet Test Scores," which profiled our Occoquan's tribes and successful state test results. When they first reached out to me, I thought it was a bit of a joke. After repeated attempts to contact me, I finally accepted a phone call to hear their initial pitch. Still a bit skeptical, I investigated further and watched a few of their short films/documentaries. Once I had actually taken the time to view their work, I was sold. The short films were edgy, clever, well put together and thought provoking. They were talking my language! When we met the next time, I said, "I'm in, on the condition we make something organic, real, authentic, gritty, and relevant." Finally, I said if they are not all-in doing it right, then I am out. In life we need to align ourselves with those who uplift us and make us better, not the other way around.

Early on, the idea was to profile my work at Occoquan and the school tribal system we had implemented. As we got going and talking, we realized there was another opportunity to tell a story with a new twist. FreeThink came along at the same time I had accepted my new position for the following school year at Fred Lynn, and we realized this was possibly the direction of the story, documenting my transition from one school to another sharing the ideas, passion, and results of my educational philosophy. As we explored this idea and concept, it kept growing with the more filming we did and the more we documented. What was awesome about the FreeThink experience was that it grew organically; there wasn't any expectation, we weren't tied to one specific concept, and it had room to breathe and develop. But the real magic was happening on an even higher level and around something more important: the people, love, and friendship. Those are the things that brought *Relentless* to life!

While making *Relentless*, I met Dusty Oakley, the mastermind behind filming and directing the film. What was really cool was that this was to be his first time directing his own film—and what an opportunity this would prove to be! Dusty is one of the most fun-loving, intelligent, reflective people I know. We shared a love for travel, exploration, and good food. We had the most amazing reflective conversations. Egos were left at the door, and we would discuss ideas and direction almost daily for *Relentless*. Dusty was always open to ideas, and the longer we spent together, the better we were able to finish each other's sentences. We wanted to change the world, disrupt the norm, and change the game with *Relentless*. We just had no idea how true this would become. Through the filming process, Dusty helped me unpack much of my anger and hate toward the way I had grown up, my parents' separation, and a whole host of other emotions that I really hadn't taken the time to unpack. Even as we climb higher mountains, we remain human. Not perfect, but chasing it, for sure. I am forever thankful that Dusty came into my world; I found a friend for life who truly, like me, cares for the world around us and wants to meaningfully impact people in a transformative way.

When you truly want to make a great documentary, it's like anything else: it takes time, effort, resources, dedication, and persistence. I quickly found out that filmmaking was no different. You don't just turn up and begin shooting and here you go. It takes hours and hours to get only a few minutes of footage; for example, *Relentless* and *Relentless 2* were put together from almost 120 hours of footage for only 9–12 minutes of film, respectively. It's an undertaking, from sound, light, lenses, environment, and endless amounts of equipment setup and breakdown. The team from FreeThink were so professional. They never got in the way and were always respectful of the types of places and times to record. We wanted to create a documentary that would truly impact others, education, and people in general. We thought *Relentless* was good, and we thought we were onto something, but what we didn't realize was how big an impact we were set to have. Over 32 million views later, *Relentless* was a viral sensation. Our story of transition, hope, and opportunity took on the world for education. Sharing it also made a profound impact on my life. Education had caught the attention of the world like never before, and Fred Lynn was officially on the map!

Upon taking over Fred Lynn, it was time to go to work, bear down, and do the work that others were not always willing and able to put their hand up to do. When everyone else was running out of the fire, I ran in. First things first. We had to follow my plan for school improvement, starting with setting about building relationships, changing mindsets, and having fun. And there's nothing like a good throw-out to start having fun again! We had truck after truck after truck pull up, load up, and throw out years and years of hoarding. It was summer holidays for students, and it was time to spring clean. It was awesome! Cleaning sent a message that there was going to be a new expectation around our building, what it looked like and felt like. During the cleanup, I found a very old flag that had been awarded to the school way back in 2003. It had been that long since we had received and experienced that level of academic excellence, more than fifteen years. I grabbed the flag and set it aside thinking, *I will use this for something motivational before the year is out.*

We got to work on appealing to the educational senses of look, touch, and feel. In went the daylight bulbs, completely brightening up the building and changing the feel. Murals went up. We changed the expectation and vocabulary of our building for students. Gone were the blank, uninspiring walls. Up went visionary leaders of the past and present, and in went the new mural of our famous boxing ring: One More Round. The school division was an amazing help during this period. We laid out a plan to fix things, things that needed updating, and maintenance that needed to take place. One by one, we knocked items off the to-do list to completely transform the building and get it ready for our students come September. In addition, we set about inventorying everything. We compiled a list of resources and set about restocking all the materials the teachers needed to be successful. We replaced old equipment all over the building. An example was the science resources we needed.

Instead of buying just cheap plastic stuff, I wanted our students to feel like scientists and ensure they had nothing but the best, so we purchased glass beakers and test tubes and other materials that helped send the message that the expectation for learning had risen.

Word spread quickly that changes were occurring, and the positive feedback flooded in the form of teachers showing up—excited and full of love—with ideas on things we could do. My answer to their suggestions was, "Green light. Let's go!" It was game on, and teachers were getting behind the movement. I dedicated every waking moment to rebuilding the confidence, love, and drive in our teachers so they could be the very best inspired version of themselves. Rather than focus on making more rules, my effort went into removing as many barriers as humanly possible, paving the way for teachers to have the green light and teach on fire again. If instruction didn't fit the expectation of being authentic and relevant, we were doing an injustice to our students who needed instruction to fit their needs and meet the expectation for a world that our students were soon to be entering as young adults. Plus when your instruction is authentic and relevant, you *feel* like you're teaching on fire. It's hard to be an amazing teacher, to be prepared to go the extra mile, but we made it worth it for the teachers because the students would quickly respond. I wanted educators to feel uplifted, valued, and respected. We treated them like the professionals they were as we worked to rebuild the culture from the bottom up. My goal was to back up the promise I had made to them that I would have their back, stand tall, and support them as educators. The only nonnegotiable was our students. I will not negotiate on their future, their outcomes, and what I expect for them. The teachers read *Fish!*, and once again I was implementing the fish philosophy as a starting point and underlying expectation for creating culture and a winning formula for all to embrace.

My effort went into removing as many barriers as humanly possible, paving the way for teachers to have the green light and teach on fire again.

1. Play.
2. Make someone's day.
3. Choose your attitude.
4. Be there.

On the first day back to school for teachers, instead of bringing them to the library to go over data, expectations, new structures, or processes, I surprised them all and put them on a bus to Washington, D.C., where we would spend the day building relationships as a staff through a scavenger hunt around the monuments of our great leaders. It was even more fun because it was a lunar eclipse, which hadn't happened in over 100 years. Even with a blistering hot day, the staff had a blast. They were troopers and came away learning new things not only about the national monuments, but more importantly, about each other. It gave us an opportunity to blend new and old staff, to get to know each other, and set new goals for the upcoming school year. We spent that entire week celebrating and uplifting one another. There were no meetings, just a focus on providing time for teachers to plan and prepare so that they could come out of the gates firing on all cylinders.

Fill the Need

Mrs. Budd-Gaspar
teacher

"I have a job offer from another school. I'm going to turn it down. I want to work for you." This was my first real interaction with Brewer. It's not as if everything's been easy since that day. Real life isn't a fairy tale. But I haven't regretted my decision.

Education is a hard field! We all know that. And having an incredible leader doesn't mean that all the hard days disappear. What it means is that on those hard days, someone has your back. When you end up in the ER and emergency surgery then out of your classroom for two months, it means your boss isn't rushing you back to school. Instead he or she is urging you to take care of yourself and offering to do anything needed to help.

It means that I'm working harder than ever to be excellent and change kids' lives. Instead of asking for permission to try something new or do things a little differently, I just do! It means that taking a unique and exciting approach to education is expected—and possible—because of the energy and atmosphere that Mr. Brewer provides.

Above all, having an outstanding leader like Hamish Brewer means that kids really do come first. Not their ability to pass "the test" and thereby prove something to the outside world. No. The mental, physical, emotional, *and* academic well-being of the child. I mean, a gym that used to be storage for broken desks now houses a top-of-the-line fitness facility! If a student has a need, he finds a way for it to be filled. The man talks a big game, and he absolutely follows through.

After that first conversation with Brewer, a skeptical coworker asked me if I was already drinking the Kool-Aid. At that time, probably not, but I had the drink poured and set out on the table. But now I'm fully invested, all-in, a true believer in the force for good in education that is Hamish Brewer.

We set the stage and counted on making a huge impact on our incoming class of sixth graders. We put a lot of work into setting the stage for a group of students who would in a couple of years become the leaders of our school. Like with anything new, some people were on board, some were not—and some were thinking about it. But we had a plan, a plan built on feedback from staff and fused with my vision for our opportunity to change the game and teach a building to love again. We delivered a set of core expectations for our entire school. In actual fact, some of the Fred Lynn staff had seen these at our old school and thought it would be a great idea to introduce, so we did. We introduced thirty essentials with the number-one expectation being "we are family." Family drives everything for me. When you can create a bond that is family, it can't be broken. When you stand up for one another, take care of one another, and fight for one another's best interests, you cannot be beaten.

The excitement became infectious, and it tied into our rebranding effort to make sure the entire world knew that there was a different conversation taking place about our school. We didn't run or hide from the old narrative; we acknowledged it, accepted it, and then used it as our fuel to change the game and disrupt the norm. We saturated our staff and community with a completely new brand, logo, and outlook. I insisted that everywhere we went we wore our swag. It was our time to become the tip of the spear and lead! We had a "Meet Mr. Brewer Night," and hundreds of people came out to find out what all the hype was about. We gave every parent a T-shirt with our new saying on the back: "Rise up!" The excitement was again contagious. Parents and students couldn't get enough, and a new day had dawned for our school. Everyone knew it was going to be different. I insisted that all the staff go to this evening event. It was early, and it was a test. I put it all on the line that if we built it, they would come, and sure enough, the families came out with all their energy and excitement, which sent a message to the staff as well: Welcome to the *new* Fred Lynn.

The most powerful motivational tool in any school is built off the backs of relationships with students. When I first started teaching, I came to realize very quickly that building a relationship is more important than any academic strategy or new technology you can bring into a classroom. It is the key component to a successful learning environment, and running a school is no different. Students come from a multitude of backgrounds, many of which would scare us. For the toughest student, they don't care about grades, they don't care about keeping a notebook, they don't care about a lot of things because for many of them, something is missing. Ultimately, they are looking for something or someone to fill a void in their life. If you want to be taken seriously as an educator, then take your students seriously. Get involved in their life and take an interest in them. For many, you may be the only person that day to say you love them or that you are proud of them.

Now that we had impacted our building, teachers, and parents, it was time to send a message to students that we were 100 percent focused on them and their learning. The teachers realized that engagement and student discipline were owned by us, the adults, and the entire culture would follow our lead.

Radical Love

Jonathan Alsheimer
teacher

When I first met Hamish Brewer, I realized very quickly that his approach to education was unique. From my experience, the only leadership I saw was behind a desk, hidden, tucked away in the corner of a school. This archaic ideology was a manuscript written from a textbook that should never be read, where academics is about test scores, data, and numbers. But Hamish Brewer was completely the opposite, understanding the sole purpose of a school is to serve children, to be an influential and positive voice for them, and to establish an environment that was cultivated by love and respect for each individual. He had an academic philosophy that said our goal is to build relationships first and from there, see our students' academic success flourish. From day one, I saw motivation being scribed onto our walls only in the ways that could resonate with our students. I saw a man riding a skateboard unapologetically different while high-fiving students. I saw a leader who wanted to interact with our students with a pure mission: to show our students his relentless love for them. He would sit with children at lunch. He held students accountable, and I saw him hold students up while they cried on his shoulder as seemingly everything in their life was crashing down upon them. I saw a true leader without hesitation go to the depths for his students. He was their advocate when they had none. He was their tangible truth. He was their influence, their positive role model, and their hope for a better future. Such powerful moments are what build a school. Powerful moments that make students realize they are more than just a number, that you love them for them, that in your eyes they are important. You are proud of them, and you will do anything for them. That is when learning happens—when radical love changed a school.

A Shot in the Arm

Mrs. Scott
teacher

By the spring of 2017, I had been working at Fred Lynn for nine years as a sixth-grade teacher and serving as the building representative for our union. Our principal was retiring, and the word on the street was we were getting the "great principal of Occoquan Elementary." I was very skeptical about Brewer. I was not open to the hype about him; he (in my opinion) was just seeking another title to add to his résumé. Would this Hamish Brewer really be there for the students and the staff of Fred Lynn? I told myself I would keep an eye on him and expose him for the true character that he really was.

Hamish Brewer is like the flu shot, and I didn't want this new medicine. I put up my wall to fight him. I was going to be a rebel and not drink his "relentless tea." But as much as I tried not to drink, he continued to be a vaccine that I may have needed after all these years. Brewer created an atmosphere where I no longer dreaded coming to work. He really cleaned and fixed some major problems in our building. Most of the staff and students fell for his infectious attitude as he stated that "We are chasing 100 at Fred Lynn." As building representative, I knew I would catch Brewer slipping and prove that he was not all-in for teachers as he had claimed. Unfortunately, I was lost for words when we would meet and discuss issues and concerns of the staff. He really listened to my suggestions, and I felt appreciated. *Damn, this guy might be all right*, I thought. No, no, he does not carry a radio or have his building keys on him all the time, and he communicates without an agenda and uses sticky notes. Brewer does not act or work like the typical principal, and I was trying to find fault in him just because he was out of the box.

To be honest, within these two years of working with Hamish Brewer, I have developed a love/hate relationship with my boss. I love that he allows me to teach my kids the way I think is best. I love that he removed the unnecessary meetings and bureaucracy that may come with managing a school. But I hate that he doesn't always answer emails, he's always somewhere in the building, and he appears to not have a written plan. He likes to go with the first idea in his head. But it's working, our students love him, the staff respects him, and so do I.

One significant issue we identified was that students were not available for learning because they were mentally checked out *or* physically absent from the classroom. The problem was resolved by three core components: supervision, instruction, and relationships. We identified that the majority of challenges were happening during transitions—and transitions are social interactions between students. To resolve those issues, we found ways to engage our students in the classroom and to be present—everywhere. Our goals were for our students to see a teacher or administrator any time they turned around. We did not have a program, for example, of greeting students at the door or being in the hallways during transition. So we made these two easily accomplishable actions a priority, and before long, student discipline issues decreased immediately. With fewer discipline issues and improved quality, tier-one, student-centered instruction, we suddenly had students more available for learning.

The visibility of the building administrators is important. It's a show of support for teachers and students. As such, I have relocated my office to a central location in the building for high visibility and student interactions. Students and teachers need to see their principals. We should not be hidden in a back corner of a school doing paperwork. We even graffitied up my office to ensure the students felt comfortable. I turned the space into a modern collaborative area for adults and students to enjoy. And even now, when I stand behind my graffitied office door as students pass by, I hear them on the other side saying things like, "He's not leaving us." For Fred Lynn, that felt like *mission accomplished!* So much goes in and out of our students' lives. I wanted to ensure that they knew I was going nowhere, that I had their back, and that I was all-in!

For the next twelve months, we would bear down and repeat the process of cleaning, upgrading, fixing, and adding to bring our school back from the brink and assure the state of Virginia we were functioning with a plan that would see us once again achieving. We would spend hours working on character education, valuing relationships between all stakeholders to rebuild our culture and school brand. As we developed our school strategy and priorities, we used the seven common traits of effective schools as a roadmap for success:

1. Acquisition of basic skills
2. Safe and orderly environment
3. High expectations
4. Strong instructional leadership
5. Pupil progress monitoring and planning
6. Authentic, relevant learning experiences
7. Fun

We had already taken care of making school safe, strong leadership, high expectations, and were on our way to setting the new standard for planning, monitoring, learning experiences, having fun, and now a basic acquisition of skills and a literacy-rich learning environment. The truth of the matter is it's not perfect, it takes time, and it won't happen overnight. The one thing that I have come to learn is that school improvement truly does take at least three years. There is no magical wand. I have just worked out the ingredients to motivate, inspire, and move the process along a bit more quickly. Hopefully from you reading this book, you too will be able to accomplish, uplift, and move your organization or school from good to great—or from failure to success.

The year was filled with so many accomplishments—none more important and more satisfying than building the relationships with the staff and most importantly the students. We celebrated regularly and began the process of rebuilding school spirit. We did this by doing something so out of the box many of our surrounding schools thought we were a little crazy. We wanted to bring families back, we wanted to fill our stands and events, so we made all the events free. Ticket sales at the gate often generate a lot of dollars toward the athletics program for example, yet we were not really making money because we were really only getting crowds at football or soccer. Once we made sporting events free, the word got out, and before we knew it, our stands for every event were packed, and our crowds were electric. What was funny is we didn't lose money. We ended up making even more because students and parents were spending money at the concessions, and with an increase in participation, we were selling out of all our products. Our sporting activities truly became events that were celebrated by our entire community.

We also completely rebranded our entire school. We raised the expectation for our brand—instead of a watered-down brand with a thousand different images and T-shirts, we went with a new image that was appropriate for middle school but gave it the first-class feel of a Division One college sports program. Our brand and image were fresh, aggressive, and classy. Our stakeholders and families loved it and got on board by buying their Hornet Nation swag. It was awesome watching the progression from the start of the year to the end when students went from wearing no Fred Lynn swag to painting their faces with school colors and wearing school shirts and swag. Unlike at the elementary level, where it was easy to get children excited about dressing up and celebrating, older kids will make the decision for themselves. They showed us they were on board!

Each month I came up with a plan to hold one or two assemblies for the students. This was a time for me to share behavior updates, set expectations, celebrate, and continue to cast the vision and mission. These assemblies were always really raw, honest, and hard hitting—if we were going to change the narrative and conversation, then we could not sugarcoat it. We had to keep it real! As students and teachers acclimated to the new expectations and order of doing things, we went for it and began to hold assemblies and celebrations for the entire school. Some people thought we were crazy for putting everyone in one place, believing that the students wouldn't behave and respond appropriately. But the students rose to the occasion, and we were able to celebrate often as an entire school.

When necessary, I would call grade-level assemblies to address events or issues. Doing so gave me a chance to make sure the students understood that we knew exactly what was going on—and exactly what would and would not be tolerated. We dealt with issues on the spot and head-on believing that for transformative change to occur, unacceptable behavior cannot be ignored or allowed to continue. When we made our expectations clear, the students quickly got on board, and the staff felt supported and valued.

Midway through the year, one of the teachers, Mr. Alsheimer, who had an MMA background, engaged a UFC fighter over social media, and before we knew it, we were on the phone with his manager working out a plan for Paul Felder to come out to Fred Lynn and possibly speak to the students. As it turned out, we went as big as ever and put on a show. We blew away Paul Felder's expectations with our fog machine, lights blacked out, and students surrounding him in the Fred Lynn Octagon. It was dynamite! He addressed the students and talked about chasing dreams and goals and about working hard inside and outside the classroom. While many people would have thought we were crazy bringing a UFC fighter in, I thought the complete opposite. He was an underdog and winner chasing championships just like us. He spoke to the values and character traits we were trying to teach the students: grit, determination, relentlessness, kindness, and going one more round! It was an outstanding success. Think big and engage your entire audience.

We teamed up with an MMA fight T-shirt company to help start an antibullying campaign. We didn't want a program that superficially addressed bullying; we wanted to address the problem head-on and to empower kids to be the answer. The Fear The Fighter apparel brand had already created some stop bullying T-shirts, and we teamed up with Chad Elliott to start a program that would make it cool to advocate for all kids. Our students, staff, and parents absolutely loved the T-shirts we created because they were current, authentic, and relevant, which is critical in pulling students into a program like this. We rewarded students with an antibullying T-shirt for helping others and for standing up to bullying. The program has been a huge hit! Schools all around the nation have followed our lead, and now businesses are jumping on board.

As the year continued to unfold, we celebrated every chance we could. If we weren't inviting the high-school bands in, then we were having fun in the hallways and classrooms—very soon, the students began to take pride and ownership of the momentum and excitement that were being generated. We were making noise, and we were putting Fred Lynn back on the map, and this energy would transfer to more engagement in the classrooms.

Our students were available for learning, and our teachers pounced on the opportunity. We started to really grow and formulate our plans for success. Our planning process began to home in and focus on what we needed to achieve success. Planning truly became a process of engagement and participation rather than an exercise of ticking the box to say you were meeting. Our processes, actions, and activities truly began to normalize, and it didn't feel like we were going from one challenge to another. By simplifying processes and having clear functional processes in place, our school was able to get back on track and operate with composure, direction, and focus.

The entire year, we were on a mission that was so layered:

- We wanted to restore respect, courage, and love to our school.
- We wanted students to engage in learning.
- We wanted teachers to love coming to work.
- Most of all, we wanted to get our school accredited again after many years of not being accredited. We did not want our school to be the one that everyone talked and wrote negatively about. We wanted to be respected again.

We lived our legacy! We rose up and showed the world that poverty and circumstances wouldn't determine our outcome. Instead of focusing on the past, we focused on the future while staying present in the moment. We didn't let anyone else tell our story or determine our outcome. We took control, and I am proud to say that every single stakeholder helped lead us to great heights. And when the day finally came, we were proud to tell the whole world that we were once again accredited.

We didn't let anyone else tell our story or determine our outcome. We took control, and I am proud to say that every single stakeholder helped lead us to great heights.

Our students have returned, and our community has given our school a vote of confidence. Our teachers feel appreciated and valued, and they love getting into the classroom and taking on the opportunity to make a difference. Students are proud to say they go to Fred Lynn, and they represent their school with pride and distinction. Alumni have reached out to show and share their support for the work that has been done. Proudly, we have shown that our school is a bright spot in the lives of our students, who feel ownership for the direction and momentum in our school. Our students prefer to be at school, hanging out with their peers and teachers. Our stadiums are full, our events are massive, and we have had an opportunity now to be the tip of the spear for education.

We have shown what the power of love can do, that poverty does not have to determine one's outcome, and a zip code will not determine the success of our school. We have taken all that is special about our school from our diversity, students, teachers, and community and turned that into fuel that has shown the world what can be done.

Our mission became even bigger and more special than we could have imagined. Our achievements impacted far more than test results; our success as a school made an impact on an entire community. We taught a school to love again. We gave a school hope. We gave a school back to its community.

We are not done. This story is far from finished. We have work to do and face a long road ahead. But we are ready to take on whatever the world dares to throw at us. We stand united, we stand relentless, and we stand together.

What is the most important thing in the world? *He tangata, he tangata, he tangata.*

It is the people, it is the people, it is the people!

People are our legacy!

10

LIVE A LIFE OF PASSION AND PURPOSE!

As a kid growing up, I would spend hours looking at the maps on my walls and the pictures of exotic locations I had cut out from magazines. I dreamed of the adventures that awaited me. I dared to imagine opportunities and possibilities, even as I worked to break out of a cycle of poverty and brokenness. Even then, I knew that life was made for living.

I never want to lose my lust for life. I don't want to look back when my time is up and have regrets. I struggle every day with the thought of growing old and my life being over. I have seen death, come close to death, and have had people die in my arms when I couldn't

I don't want to look back on my life at the end of it and wonder *what if?*

save them. I don't want to look back on my life at the end of it and wonder *what if?*

It's easy to get lost in our routines and careers and lose our way. We slip into unhealthy lifestyles that become unbalanced and focused on living to work rather than working to live and enjoying life. It's important to look at life and make sure we are doing more of the things that we want to do, not just should do. We have to be intentional to make time to enjoy the simple things, to take care of ourselves. I tell my staff often, "No work this weekend! Go out and do something for yourself!" As educators, we give so much of ourselves to other people's children and to our communities that it's easy to forget to nourish and reenergize ourselves. Even as we are proud to serve others, we have to take care of ourselves as well. So let's be intentional about living with purpose and passion. Let's be intentional about planning time to do the things we've always dreamed of.

Look into the eyes of your students and notice the wide-eyed wonder they have about the possibilities life holds for them. When does that fade? Where does that wonder go? All too often, people place their dreams on hold and end up losing sight of them. Maybe you've made a bucket list and then tucked it away in a book and forgotten about it. When you shelve your dreams for "another day" or "for when I get time," you fall into the trap of thinking they could never happen. Stop and ask yourself, *Why not?* Why not me? Why not continue to chase my dreams as an adult? Why not now? By going after your dreams, you are a model for the people in your life, giving them hope that maybe they can and should pursue their greatest wishes.

Life is a journey. It's full of seasons. Our paths take us all in different directions, and as we focus on the end goal, we forget to love the process. Embrace your journey—right now—because this is where the soul lives. It lives in the hard work, learning from our mistakes and from failing. It thrives in the moments when we get back up and go one more round. The best journeys in life bring us to new learning about ourselves—about our soul and passion. These journeys often yield more questions than answers, but with this comes opportunity. So embrace the journey, embrace the experience, and don't let anyone else dictate the person or life you wish to lead. I'll tell you what I tell my students: Do not let anyone steal your future!

Dreams don't come true without a plan and without taking action. Start today to take a small step toward your dream. Start making your plan for doing something fun and exciting or maybe just doing something simple and small for yourself.

Don't wait until something significant happens in your life to make the changes you want to make or to do those things you have always wanted to do. All too often, people wait until they have let themselves go and the doctor sounds the wake-up call, or until they have lost a loved one, or until the midlife crisis hits. I'm telling you right now: there is no better time than the present to take charge, take control, and live the life you always wished to live.

The reality check here is that you know the mistakes you are making. You know the toxic, negative mindset you can get yourself into. Give up the excuses! Your life is up to you. Take charge, take back your time, put down your phone, and focus on the direction you want to go and the person you want to be. You don't want to look back with regrets, wondering about the what-ifs that could have been. This is your time to shed the fear and be unapologetically relentless. Stop thinking and talking about what you want to do. Talk is cheap. What happens next is completely up to you. So let's go. Mount up!

I have worked on my bucket list for years. It's a list of the things I want to see and do before I die. I have accomplished some of the items on my list, and some are yet to be realized. Some are lofty, and some are easy. But none of the items on my list has happened or will happen without intentional action.

I challenge you to create your own bucket list. Write down the things you have always wanted to do or only dreamed about. Include the things that you feel you have accomplished and done. Share it with a loved one. I encourage you to try this activity with your staff and students. It's something they will enjoy, and it will provide you an opportunity to learn more about them. If you have a partner or children, ask them what they would put on their bucket list. And then go make it happen!

You have permission to live a life of passion and purpose. Dare to be different; dare to be bold! Be the best you!

THE RELENTLESS, TATTOOED, SKATEBOARDING PRINCIPAL'S BUCKET LIST

1. PLAY A SET AT A RAVE.

2. TRAVEL THE TRANS-SIBERIAN RAILWAY.

3. CLIMB MACHU PICCHU.

4. SING IN A MUSICAL.

5. BASE JUMP.

6. BUILD A RAT ROD.

7. ~~SKYDIVE.~~

8. ~~HAVE A VIRAL VIDEO.~~

9. MEET TONY HAWK.

10. BACKPACK AROUND THE WORLD. HALFWAY THERE.

11. ~~MAKE A DOCUMENTARY.~~

12. STAND ON EVERY CONTINENT.

13. FLY IN A WORLD WAR II SPITFIRE.

14. HANG OUT WITH ROB DYRDEK.

15. TRANSFORM AN INDUSTRIAL BUILDING INTO A RESIDENTIAL ONE.

16. BUILD A SCHOOL.

17. ~~DANCE IN THE RAIN.~~

18. ~~PAY FOR SOMEONE'S GROCERIES.~~

19. SWIM WITH TURTLES.

20. SAIL AROUND THE WORLD.

21. PERFORM THE HAKA WITH THE ALL BLACKS.

22. ~~FALL IN LOVE.~~

23. ~~BECOME A FIREMAN.~~

24. ~~LIVE WITH PASSION.~~

25. STOP POLLUTION.

26. PROVIDE FRESH WATER TO EVERYONE.

27. ~~GO INSIDE A PYRAMID.~~

28. MAKE A TRAVEL EDUCATION SHOW.

29. SWIM WITH SHARKS.

30. HANG OUT WITH OBAMA.

31. BE ON THE ELLEN SHOW.

32. CHARGE ONTO THE FIELD AND GET AWAY WITH IT.

33. DRIVE FROM THE TOP OF NORTH AMERICA TO BOTTOM OF SOUTH AMERICA.

34. TRAVEL THE PANAMA CANAL.

35. ~~ROCK CLIMB IN ASIA.~~

36. PARTY WITH SOMEONE FAMOUS.

37. HANG OUT WITH A SNIPER.

38. BE FEATURED IN A MAGAZINE.

39. ~~WRITE A BOOK.~~

40. RUN WITH THE BULLS.

41. LIVE IN A CASTLE.

42. START A NONPROFIT.

43. LEARN TO FLY A PLANE.

44. WALK THE RED CARPET.

45. LEAD A PROTEST.

46. STAND ON THE SOUTH POLE.

47. GET A DOCTORATE. ALMOST THERE.

48. CHANGE A COMMUNITY.

49. TURN A SCHOOL AROUND.

50. THROW A FIRST PITCH OUT AT A YANKEES' GAME.

51. CRASH A WEDDING.

52. GET MARRIED.

53. GET A RIDE WITH THE BLUE ANGELS.

54. HELP A FRIEND IN NEED.

55. RUN THE SPEIGHTS COAST TO COAST.

56. MISS A PLANE.

57. TRAVEL FIRST CLASS.

58. RUN A HALF AND FULL MARATHON. COMPLETED A HALF.

59. GO ICE FISHING.

60. GROW DREADLOCKS. (MAY HAVE MISSED THE BOAT.)

61. WEAR A KILT IN SCOTLAND.

62. HANG OUT WITH JACK JOHNSON.

63. BUILD A SCHOOL IN A VILLAGE.

64. COAST-TO-COAST BASEBALL ROAD TRIP.

65. STAY IN AN ICE HOTEL.

66. PERFORM ON STAGE WITH COLDPLAY.

67. GET SCUBA CERTIFICATION.

68. THROW A SURPRISE PARTY.

69. GO TO MT. EVEREST.

70. QUIT MY JOB.

71. TAKE STUDENTS TO THE WHITE HOUSE.

72. BECOME A MOTIVATIONAL SPEAKER.

73. WALK THE GREAT WALL OF CHINA.

74. BUILD A TREEHOUSE.

75. DRINK A GUINNESS IN IRELAND.

76. RIDE WITH A MOTORCYCLE CLUB.

77. TRAIN WITH NAVY SEALS.

78. VISIT THE SEVEN WONDERS OF THE WORLD.

79. ADVOCATE FOR EDUCATION.

80. SAVE CHILDREN'S LIVES...

81. CLEAN PLASTIC FROM OCEAN.

82. PARTY ON IBIZA.

83. TELL PEOPLE I LOVE THEM.

84. THROW TOMATOES IN SPAIN.

85. GO TO SPACE.

86. I WANT TO THANK MY PARENTS.

87. BE ON A LATE-NIGHT SHOW WITH JAMES CORDON.

88. CHANGE SOMEONE'S LIFE.

89. FLY IN A HOT-AIR BALLOON.

90. LEARN ANOTHER LANGUAGE.

91. ELIMINATE BULLYING.

92. TRAVEL IN A VOLKSWAGEN KOMBI VAN FOR A YEAR.

93. CLIMB A GLACIER.

94. DONATE TO COMMUNITY PROJECTS.

95. DO A TED TALK.

96. SPEND A DAY ON AN AIRCRAFT CARRIER.

97. HELP A STRANGER.

98. FIND PEACE.

99. FIND HAPPINESS.

100. KNOW I MADE A DIFFERENCE.

ACKNOWLEDGMENTS

It would be an injustice to leave anyone out as I have so many people to say thank you to and to acknowledge for their part in my life's journey.

To Jason, Sue, and the Ng family—Thank you for saving my life, taking me into your home and family during my darkest hour, and for reminding me about living a life with passion and purpose.

Thank you to everyone who contributed to my book in big and small ways via support: the firehouse, those in New Zealand, and those who wrote the excerpts that we are all getting to enjoy.

To Andy Jacks—Thank you for always keeping it real, being there for me no matter the circumstances, and pushing me to be better every day! Let's keep having fun and going on adventures together!

To my family, Dad, Mum, Cameron, and Duncan—Life has had its ups and downs, but we are finally at peace with what happened and with each other. I know none of us would change much when we look back; it made us all who we are today. Regardless of how life transpired, we are all closer now than ever before and living a life filled with love, passion, and purpose!

To my family Ashley, Ava, Zara, Perry, and Sawyer—You have all sacrificed more than anyone will know so that I can do the thing I am so passionate about! Ashley, you have stood by me from the very first time we met. I knew then, as I still know today, that you were the one!

MORE FROM

DAVE BURGESS Consulting, Inc.

Since 2012, DBCI has been publishing books that inspire and equip educators to be their best. For more information on our DBCI titles or to purchase bulk orders for your school, district, or book study, visit **DaveBurgessConsulting.com/DBCIBooks**.

More from the *Like a PIRATE*™ Series

Teach Like a PIRATE by Dave Burgess

Explore Like a Pirate by Michael Matera

Learn Like a Pirate by Paul Solarz

Play Like a Pirate by Quinn Rollins

Run Like a Pirate by Adam Welcome

***Lead Like a PIRATE*™ Series**

Lead Like a PIRATE by Shelley Burgess and Beth Houf

Balance Like a Pirate by Jessica Cabeen, Jessica Johnson, and Sarah Johnson

Lead with Culture by Jay Billy

Lead with Literacy by Mandy Ellis

Lead beyond Your Title by Nili Bartley

Leadership & School Culture

Culturize by Jimmy Casas

Escaping the School Leader's Dunk Tank by Rebecca Coda
and Rick Jetter

The Innovator's Mindset by George Couros

Kids Deserve It! by Todd Nesloney and Adam Welcome

Let Them Speak! by Rebecca Coda and Rick Jetter

Start. Right. Now. by Todd Whitaker, Jeffrey Zoul, and
Jimmy Casas

Stop. Right. Now. by Jimmy Casas and Jeffrey Zoul Jetter

The Limitless School by Abe Hege and Adam Dovico

The Pepper Effect by Sean Gaillard

The Principled Principal by Jeffrey Zoul and
Anthony McConnell

The Secret Solution by Todd Whitaker, Sam Miller, and
Ryan Donlan

They Call Me "Mr. De" by Frank DeAngelis

Unmapped Potential by Julie Hasson and Missy Lennard

Your School Rocks by Ryan McLane and Eric Lowe

Technology & Tools

50 Things You Can Do with Google Classroom by Alice Keeler
and Libbi Miller

50 Things to Go Further with Google Classroom by Alice Keeler
and Libbi Miller

140 Twitter Tips for Educators by Brad Currie, Billy Krakower,
and Scott Rocco

Code Breaker by Brian Aspinall

Creatively Productive by Lisa Johnson

Google Apps for Littles by Christine Pinto and Alice Keeler

Master the Media by Julie Smith

Shake Up Learning by Kasey Bell

Social LEADia by Jennifer Casa-Todd

Teaching Math with Google Apps by Alice Keeler and
  Diana Herrington
TeachingLand by Amanda Fox and Mary Ellen Weeks

Teaching Methods & Materials
All 4s and 5s by Andrew Sharos
Ditch That Homework by Matt Miller and Alice Keeler
Ditch That Textbook by Matt Miller
EDrenaline Rush by John Meehan
Educated by Design by Michael Cohen
The EduProtocol Field Guide by Marlena Hebern and
  Jon Corippo
Instant Relevance by Denis Sheeran
LAUNCH by John Spencer and A.J. Juliani
Make Learning MAGICAL by Tisha Richmond
Pure Genius by Don Wettrick
Shift This! by Joy Kirr
Spark Learning by Ramsey Musallam
Sparks in the Dark by Travis Crowder and Todd Nesloney
Table Talk Math by John Stevens
The Classroom Chef by John Stevens and Matt Vaudrey
The Wild Card by Hope and Wade King
The Writing on the Classroom Wall by Steve Wyborney

Inspiration, Professional Growth, & Personal Development
Be REAL by Tara Martin
Be the One for Kids by Ryan Sheehy
The EduNinja Mindset by Jennifer Burdis
Empower Our Girls by Lynmara Colón and Adam Welcome
The Four O'Clock Faculty by Rich Czyz

How Much Water Do We Have? by Pete and Kris Nunweiler

P Is for Pirate by Dave and Shelley Burgess

The Path to Serendipity by Allyson Apsey

Through the Lens of Serendipity by Allyson Apsey

Sanctuaries by Dan Tricarico

Shattering the Perfect Teacher Myth by Aaron Hogan

Stories from Webb by Todd Nesloney

Talk to Me by Kim Bearden

The Zen Teacher by Dan Tricarico

Children's Books

Dolphins in Trees by Aaron Polansky

The Princes of Serendip by Allyson Apsey

INVITE HAMISH BREWER TO YOUR NEXT PROFESSIONAL DEVELOPMENT EVENT

Hamish is an international keynote speaker, speaking on a variety of topics targeting educators, students, leaders, emergency responders, and businesses all around the world. Here are a few of the topics he covers:

Legacy

People want to be part of something special, something bigger than themselves. This motivational presentation will completely change your perspective on life, business, and education. Hamish's message will challenge you to be better, to make those around you better, and to leave an impact on world through your legacy. Come on a journey that will inspire you to chase greatness!

Relentless

Sometimes you have to hear the things you don't want to hear in order to move forward, to be better, and to get results. Hamish will take you on a hard-hitting journey that will challenge you to rethink your practices, disrupt the norm, and change the game. Do you have what it takes to go one more round? Are you willing to advocate for every single person in your life? Hamish will push you to dig deep and to be relentless in the pursuit of taking your school or organization to the next level.

School Improvement

Learn from an award-winning leader and school turnaround expert who has worked with some of America's most at-risk students in schools at both the elementary and secondary levels. In this presentation, Hamish share the secrets to his schools' successes. You'll learn how to use research and proven practices to improve your culture, instruction, and processes to get real results!

Culture

Is your school, school division, or business suffering from a toxic environment? Do you need to uplift the culture—before it's too late? Hamish will help you reignite the magic of your students and staff by sharing authentic and relevant experiences that you can implement immediately!

Literacy

Hamish shares his results and experiences in creating an award-winning literacy program from the ground up. You'll learn how to address the needs of all learners while closing the achievement gap. From the book room to the classroom and into students' homes, you'll learn how to make reading part of your school's culture and improve results—even with the most at-risk learners.

Leadership

Are you an aspiring leader, a new leader, or a leader who just wants to rethink the way you work? If so, this session with Hamish will walk you through how to get leadership right—right from the beginning. You'll learn how to avoid making common mistakes and how to develop your necessary leadership skills, such as communication and decision-making. You'll walk away with a vision for creating an award-winning school or business.

Have the Life You've Always Dreamed Of!

In this session for high-school students, Hamish focuses on building a legacy and a life. As he shares about his own failings and the struggles he faced in high school, he inspires students to set themselves up for success and equips them with the skills they'll need to take on the world.

Living a Life of Passion and Purpose!

What's your dream? What's on your bucket list? Hamish encourages you to dig deep into yourself and identify what you *really* want. From here, he offers encouragement to help you live a life of passion and purpose as you make those dreams come true.

Emergency Response—Notes from the Field

As a former fireman and emergency responder, Hamish delivers this keynote based on his experiences in the field, the front seat, and in leadership in extreme environments. For those who work daily to rescue people despite serious risks, this session offers incredible motivation and encouragement.

HamishBrewer.com

ABOUT THE AUTHOR

Hamish Brewer, the relentless, tattooed, skateboarding principal in northern Virginia, isn't your typical principal. Hamish is high octane, constantly calling on his students to "Be relentless." He has become known as an educational disrupter who transcends the status quo and typical educational norms.

Hamish serves at the state level as the federal relations coordinator on the board of directors with the Virginia Association of Elementary School Principals. He is a school turnaround and school improvement specialist, working with some of the most at-risk students in the United States. Under his leadership, his elementary school was recognized as a Nationally Distinguished Title I School. He has since gone on to turn around one of the toughest middle schools in the state of Virginia.

Originally from New Zealand, Hamish spent years developing and honing his leadership and expertise as an emergency responder in the fire and rescue service, working at one of the busiest volunteer fire stations on the Eastern seaboard. In additional to serving as a middle-school principal today, he is a highly sought-after international keynote and TEDx speaker who motivates and inspires audiences. He has been highlighted as a Hometown Hero by Fox 5 in Washington, D.C. With more than 32 million views, the *Relentless* story has become a viral sensation being featured on the national news broadcasts, including with NBC and Lester Holt. He is also being featured in the skateboarding humanitarian documentary, *Humanity Stoked.*

Hamish was recognized in 2017 as the NAESP Nationally Distinguished Principal and Virginia Principal of the Year. He has also been recognized as the 2016 VAESP School Bell Award and ASCD Virginia Impact Award. In 2018, Hamish was named a Northern Virginian of the Year by *Northern Virginia Magazine* and the 2018 Principal of the Year by *Education Dive.* Prince William County Public Schools named him the 2019 Principal of the Year.